# Lost in the Meritocracy

## Also by Walter Kirn

# Lost in the Meritocracy

## The Undereducation of an Overachiever

# Walter Kirn

DOUBLEDAY

New York    London    Toronto    Sydney    Auckland

**DD**
**DOUBLEDAY**

Published in the United States by Doubleday, a division of Random House, Inc., New York.
www.doubleday.com

The author and publisher gratefully acknowledge the *Atlantic* and the *New York Times* "Education Life," in which parts of this book were originally published.

DOUBLEDAY and the DD colophon are registered trademarks of Random House, Inc.

*Book design by Donna Sinisgalli*

Library of Congress Cataloging-in-Publication Data
Kirn, Walter, 1962–
Lost in the meritocracy : the undereducation of an overachiever / by Walter Kirn.
—1st ed.
     p. cm.
1. Kirn, Walter, 1962—Childhood and youth. 2. Authors, American—20th century—Biography. 3. Authors, American—21st century—Biography. 4. Students—United States—Biography. I. Title.
  PS3561.I746Z46  2009
  813'.54—dc22
  [B]

                                                    2008051075

ISBN 978-0-385-52128-4

PRINTED IN THE UNITED STATES OF AMERICA

10  9  8  7  6  5  4  3  2  1

First Edition

*This is a work of memory concerning events from more than twenty-five years ago. It attempts to be truthful in its narrative. There are, I suspect, a number of inaccuracies, but no deliberate deceptions. Out of regard for their privacy, several individuals' names have been changed and their identities disguised.*

—WALTER KIRN

To the humane and dedicated educators who helped me find my way when I could barely see the path: Joyce Carol Oates, James Richardson, Seth Lerer, J. D. McClatchy, Alvin Greenberg, and Neil Rudenstine. To Robert Vare and the *Atlantic* for giving this book its start in their pages. And with gratitude to my unstintingly tough-minded and charmingly forbearing editor, Gerry Howard, a true man of letters in the grand old manner.

I tell myself it all seems like fun and will work out in the end. I expect I will be asked a question I can answer and then be handed a big prize. They're working on it.

—JOHN ASHBERY,
"THE ICE STORM"

I see now that this has been a story of the West, after all—Tom and Gatsby, Daisy and Jordan and I, were all Westerners, and perhaps we possessed some deficiency in common which made us subtly unadaptable to Eastern life.

—F. SCOTT FITZGERALD,
*THE GREAT GATSBY*

# Lost in the Meritocracy

ON THE BUS RIDE DOWN TO ST. PAUL TO TAKE THE TEST that will help determine who will get ahead in life, who will stay put, and who will fall behind, a few of my closest buddies seal their fates by opening pint bottles of cherry schnapps the moment we leave the high-school parking lot. My pals hide the liquor under their varsity jackets and monitor the driver's overhead mirror for opportune moments to duck their heads and swig. A girl sees what they're up to, mutters "Morons," and goes back to shading in the tiny ovals in her Scholastic Aptitude Test review book. She dated one of the guys awhile back and seemed amused by his clowning for a time, but lately she's grown serious, ambitious; I've heard she's decided to practice law someday and prosecute companies that pollute the air. When she notices one of the bottles coming my way, she shoots me a look of horror.

"No thanks," I say.

My friends seem wounded by this—aren't we teammates? We play football and baseball together. We hang out. In our high-school class there are only fifteen boys, and every summer before the bugs get bad a bunch of us pitch tents beside the river and cannonball from the cliffs into the current, sometimes splashing down in twos and threes. In the winters some of us work at the same ski hill, selling lift tickets and running chair-lifts, and during haying season we form crews to help out the guys who live on farms. We talk as though we'll be together for-ever, but I've always known better: someday we'll be ranked. We'll be screened and scored and separated. I've known this, it seems, since my first few years in grade school, not in this town, Taylors Falls, but in Marine, a few miles down the valley, when I raised my hand slightly faster than the other kids—and waved it around to make sure the teachers saw me.

A friend pushes the schnapps on me again just as I'm start-ing to panic about time. The test begins in an hour and a half but we're still twenty minutes from the interstate, stuck behind a lumbering Case tractor in the land of grain silos and barns where my family lives on a small farm that we cultivate, Amish style, with a team of horses, and where I spend my after-school hours splitting firewood, setting fence posts, filling stock tanks, and collecting eggs. It's been my home for several years now, but it's also a stage set, a fantasy, and one that I've never found con-vincing. My father isn't a farmer, he's a patent lawyer, and our family's excursion into vintage agriculture (like our conversion to Mormonism, which preceded it) is just one more phase in his campaign against convention and conformity that began twelve years ago, when he joined the 3M Corporation in St. Paul and sacrificed, as he saw it, his sacred freedom to the dictates of the herd. He's been rebelling ever since, pursuing a rugged individ-ualism that has involved, at different times, bow hunting, moun-tain climbing, weight lifting, and now, in his greatest caprice to date, nineteenth-century subsistence living. But those days are almost over, at least for me. I gaze out the bus window at the countryside and wonder what could have drawn my father here other than an instinct for self-punishment. Junk cars up on cinder blocks in scrubby fields, mangled deer on the shoulders of dirt roads, lonely old folks sitting on sagging porches breathing from portable tanks of oxygen. I see myself living in New York someday, in an art-filled apartment with views of vaulting bridges, not mired in this place of wistful rot.

"I already said I don't want any," I say. The guy now holding out the schnapps is named Rolf, a hulking colossus of pale Norwegian gristle who plays center on the Bluejays, our losing football team.

"Afraid you'll catch my germs?" he cracks.

"Everybody who drinks from the school water fountain already has your germs."

"Right. Like you're some perfect Mr. Clean."

"At least I shake off before I zip back up."

Rolf flips me the bird. There's black crud under his fingernails. He works part-time for his uncle's excavation company, and once he learns to run a diesel backhoe he'll have job security for life. Instead of wasting my energy sparring with him, I should be concentrating on the review book like the red-haired boy across from me, the only other A student on the bus. He's a hard kid to get to know, a social ghost, forbidden by his family's harsh religion from singing holiday-related songs and forced by its stringent dietary teachings to live on sack lunches of carrots and slivered almonds. Sometimes I fear he's brighter than I am; he's certainly more studious. He works with his head down, calm and dogged, while I rely on gimmicky maneuvers such as

rephrasing teachers' simple questions ("How does racial prejudice contribute to inner-city hopelessness?") into complicated
riddles ("Is our conception of 'inner-city hopelessness' perhaps
in *itself* a form of prejudice?") designed to provoke class discussions that I can dominate with my amped-up flash-card-based
vocabulary. Do my ploys show intelligence or desperation?
Both, I suspect. In me the traits seem fused.

I watch the bottle being passed and I make my final plea.

"Stop it, you guys. Today is a big deal for us."

But they know this already—they just don't like the fact.
The SAT isn't a reckoning they asked for. The exam was devised
by strangers on the East Coast, a part of the country we associate
with stockbrokers, mobsters, and fashion models. The sample
questions in the review books (ART : CUBISM : : (A) scenery :
play; (B) setting : ring; (C) mustache : face; (D) poem : epic) resemble none we've ever faced. Taylors Falls Public High School
is a dump. Grades K through twelve are stuffed into one squat
building surrounded by crabgrass ball fields full of gopher holes,
and some of our teachers do little but coach sports. They wear
their whistles and ball caps at their desks, paging through magazines while we, their students, pass the class hours scribbling in
photocopied "workbooks" whose fuzzy type and off-key phras-
ings ("Among the proud peoples of the Orient . . .") suggest that
they haven't been updated for decades.

The St. Paul skyline stands up in the windshield as one of
my classmates flings back a shot of schnapps and licks his sticky
lips. "Nice little head rush. Try it, Walt. Come on." He holds
the bottle by its neck and swings it in front of me like a hypno-
tist's pocket watch. "Getting thirsty. Getting very thirsty . . ."

The numbskulls around him pretend they're going under, drooping their heads and fluttering their eyelids.

"A sip," someone says. "Just one," says someone else.

I shake my head. "I'm sorry. No."

And so I go on to college, and they don't.


**P**ercentile is destiny in America.

Four years after that bus ride to the testing center, I'm slumped on a shabby sofa in the library of a Princeton University eating club, waiting to feel the effects of two black capsules that someone said would help me finish writing my overdue application for a Rhodes Scholarship. I'm chain-smoking, too, and I have been for an hour—Marlboro Lights with their filters twisted off, whose butts I drop into a can of Dr Pepper spiked with Smirnoff vodka. I'm seven pounds lighter than I was in high school but not as trim and perhaps not quite as tall, my center of gravity having sunk closer to chair level. I need glasses, too. I doubt that the cause is too much reading, though; thanks to my flair for academic shortcuts and an impression I've gained from certain professors that the Great Books are not as great as advertised (and may indeed be pernicious instruments of social manipulation and oppression), I've done much less reading here than I expected. No, I blame my dimming vision, as I do my sagging physique and my reliance on chemical pick-me-ups, on a gradual neurological withdrawal from a place that no longer seemed to want me once it decided, by some fluke, to have me.

"You sure you took both of them?" my close friend Adam asks. What's making him wonder is the blank legal pad resting on my lap. I should be writing furiously by now, but instead I'm compulsively clicking my ballpoint pen and nibbling a cold blister on my lower lip.

"Maybe the pills were counterfeit," I say.

"You haven't absorbed them. Your stomach's full from dinner."

"I missed dinner. All I ate was tapioca."

"Tapioca would do it," Adam says.

I trust his theory; he knows his physiology. A Jewish science whiz from the New York suburbs, he ate magic mushrooms one evening, had a vision (matter is not composed of atoms but infinitesimal knots of thought), and switched the next day from premed to English literature. He ought to be reading James Joyce's *Dubliners*, which he'll be tested on this week, but instead he's conducting an experiment: grinding up Percocet tablets in a soup bowl and trying to smoke the powder through a water pipe. He flicks the wheel of his lighter with a thumb and steadies the flame above the pipe's bronze bowl. When the powder liquifies, browns, and starts to bubble, he sucks up the vapors with a mighty gasp that causes me to hold my breath in sympathy.

I have other comrades in estrangement, way out here on the bell curve's leading edge, where our talent for multiple-choice tests has landed us without even the vaguest survival instructions. Our club isn't one of the rich, exclusive outfits, where the pedigreed children of the Establishment eat chocolate-dipped strawberries off silver trays delivered by black waiters in starched white uniforms, but one that anyone can join, where screwballs and misfits line up with plastic trays for veggie burgers and canned fruit salad. At the moment the club is floundering financially and has fewer than twenty paid-up members, including two religious fanatics who came to Princeton as normal young men, I'm told, but failed for some reason to mix and grew eccentric. Not many months from now, one will interpret a Bible passage too literally and try to pluck out his left eye in penance for some failing he won't disclose. The other will style himself a campus prophet and try to persuade a dozen "disciples"—most of them urban black kids, here on aid—to renounce their degrees just prior to graduation as a way to appease a wrathful God bent on smiting the campus with holy fire. I get along with this junior Jeremiah thanks to my experience with Mormonism, which accustomed me to apocalyptic small talk.

"Why will the Lord strike Princeton first?" I ask him. "Why not the White House, say, or New York City?"

"I'm only the messenger. I don't ask questions."

"What about Yale and Harvard?"

"They're no concern of mine."

"This came to you how, this warning? In a dream?"

"I was trying to solve a set-theory equation when suddenly I started writing in Hebrew."

Others in the club are less expressive. They keep to themselves, tight-lipped and self-contained. One kid, a token North Dakotan (Princeton likes to boast that it has students from all fifty states), wears the same greaser haircut he brought from Bismarck and has poured all his energy for years into fronting a lackadaisical rock band specializing in heavy-metal anthems that were popular in my town, too, but which the smart set has taught me to disdain in favor of morbid British art-pop by groups such as Public Image and Joy Division. The North Dakota kid never changed his tastes, though, and part of me envies his stubbornness. Joy Division, to my ears, isn't music. It's more like the noise in a coma victim's brain.

A few of my club mates scare me. I avoid them. One, a reputed physics prodigy, is catatonic from LSD, which he takes by placing the tabs on his bare eyeballs. On weekends he engages in pinball marathons that sometimes last ten hours. Strike a match an inch from his face and he won't flinch—his pupils won't even contract. Then there's the girl in the neck brace whom we call Anna, after the heroine of Tolstoy's novel. A comp-lit student, pale and heavyset, she told Adam one night at dinner that they were destined to be married. She said he reminded her of Vronsky, the dashing army officer who, in the novel, captures Anna's heart but eventually wanes in his devotion, leading to her suicide. When Adam asked the girl to go away, she flung herself off a third-floor metal railing in the atrium of his dormitory. She survived, by some miracle, and ever since Adam has been her guilty slave, buttering her toast at breakfast, keeping her coffee cup topped up, and reading out loud to her from Dostoyevsky, her new favorite writer, which may spell doom for both of them.

"Feeling the buzz yet?" he asks me.

I shake my head.

"So what are the two best stories in *Dubliners*?"

"The last one, supposedly, 'The Dead,' which ends with an image of falling snow that's meant to symbolize mortality, and 'Araby,' the one about a boy who sneaks out to a carnival, spends all his money, and then slinks home to bed, totally overcome by shame."

"Shame about what?"

"Just shame. It's irreducible."

"You actually read that somewhere or you just thought it? I don't want to get shot down on this."

"You won't be. 'Irreducible' is foolproof."

If my buddies from Minnesota could see me now, they wouldn't have a clue whom they were seeing, and I wouldn't be able to help them. Four years ago my SAT scores launched a new phase in a trajectory that I'd been riding since age five. One morning I opened a test sheet filled with questions concerning synonyms and antonyms and the meeting times of trucks in opposite lanes, and the next thing I knew I was showered with fawning letters from half the colleges in the country. Macalester College, in St. Paul, made me a singularly tempting offer: immediate admission as a freshman. I didn't even have to finish high school. I accepted their invitation, but my plan was not to stay. In imitation of F. Scott Fitzgerald, Minnesota's most famous writer and the author of *The Great Gatsby*, the only serious work of literature that I managed to finish as a teenager, I wanted to go East. I wanted to ride the train to the last station. A natural-born child of the meritocracy, I'd been amassing momentum my whole life, entering spelling bees, vying for forensics medals, running my mouth in mock United Nations, and I knew only one direction: forward. I lived for prizes, plaques, citations, stars, and I gave no thought to any goal beyond my next appearance on the honor roll. Learning was secondary, promotion was primary. No one ever told me what the point was, except to keep on accumulating points, and this struck me as sufficient. What else was there?

Before I'd been at Macalester a month, I applied to transfer to Princeton as a sophomore. It's here I should note that my father went there, too, although he never encouraged me to follow him or showed much interest in my college plans generally. A middle-class son of Akron, Ohio, possessed of a girder-like physique and a lust for brutal contact sports, he'd been recruited to play football by Princeton, Harvard, Yale, and a number of other institutions, many of them based in the Midwest and which he was unaware held less prestige until a friend of his family clued him in about the mythos of the Ivy League—a designation my father understood as mostly athletic-related, like the Big Ten. He chose Princeton over the other schools because his father was jobless at the time and the university's recruiter offered not only to cover his tuition but also to excuse him from the work requirement that was standard with scholarship recipients. As for the four years that followed, he rarely spoke of them, except to mention he'd drunk a lot of beer, majored in chemistry, and felt out of place at first as a public-school kid. That was the sum of it. No nostalgic stories, no romantic reminiscences. He'd made a few friends at Princeton but rarely saw them, keeping in touch through occasional phone calls, and when mail came that bore the Princeton logo, it usually wound up, unopened, in the trash.

Applying to Princeton was my idea alone. It came to me on a bike ride down Summit Avenue, just a few blocks from the Macalester campus, when I used a map from a professor to locate F. Scott Fitzgerald's boyhood home. It wasn't the mansion I'd expected. In fact, it looked like a house I might have lived in had my father not quarantined us on the farm. A few days later I got my nerve up and phoned the Princeton admissions office, from which I learned that the university took only twenty transfer students a year. This was a discouraging statistic, but I was used to being the exception: it was the only condition I'd ever known.

To bolster my application, I looked around Macalester for a contest, any contest, that I might place first in, hitting at last on a poetry competition that seemed to be attracting few entries. I'd never written poetry before, but I knew something of how serious poems should look (ragged, chaotic, with uneven lines) thanks to a paperback volume of "free verse" loaned to me by a pothead high-school English teacher who'd once had ambitions as a writer but gave them up when he got his girlfriend pregnant.

Here is what I wrote:

From an Uncolored Room
*Morning is a confrontation with the visible*
*and the bold verdicts of utility.*
*The toothpaste tube on the sink like a beached fish,*
*the face in the toilet water.*

*At breakfast I depress the toast,*
*but turn away, determined not to notice*
*the hot bread swaying briefly in its slots*
*between the red wires.*

*It rains, and I am reminded*
*I have lost all respect for the weather,*
*which allows itself to be predicted*
*and visits the city purely out of habit*
*but changes nothing*

*for men who can throw off gods and loved ones*
*like cats from their laps.*


*When my brother left on Tuesday*
*I pushed the beds together.*
*I sleep on the crack.*


When I won the contest, I wasn't surprised. Hunger, I'd learned, could be a form of genius.

Nor was I surprised a few months later when I found myself sitting in a Princeton lecture hall that was older than my hometown, writing down a new word: "post-structuralism." I couldn't define the term—no one could, it seemed, including much of the English Department faculty—but I knew more or less what it meant: I'd broken through. The student beside me bore a famous last name that I recognized from a history textbook (not Rockefeller, but close), and discovering that the name was still in use among living individuals—people whom I was expected to befriend now and make a life and career among, if possible—renewed in me a sense of dislocation that I'd been struggling with since I entered school.

Three years later, high on speed and applying for the Rhodes, I'm feeling more disoriented than ever. Late last winter, about eight months ago, I simply ran out of thoughts. I ran out of the stuff that thoughts are made of. I became mute, aphasic. I couldn't write. I couldn't process human speech. A doctor I saw pronounced me deeply malnourished and prescribed a regimen of vitamins, but my depletion was spiritual, I sensed, and also—it seemed possible—permanent. I'd been fleeing upward since age five, learning just enough at every level to make it, barely, to the next one. I was the system's pure product, sly and flexible, not so much educated as wised up, but suddenly I hit a wall.

Adam passes me the water pipe, its bowl freshly packed with pulverized narcotics. He clicks the lighter. "It's not like you'll see the face of God," he says, "but it does sort of turn your legs all warm and rubbery."

I fill my lungs and flash back to that bus ride, to the beckoning bottles of cherry schnapps. Back then I knew where I was going, and that to get there I'd have to keep my head clear. But now I'm here, I've arrived, I've topped the hill, and my head doesn't function the way it used to. All thanks to an education and a test that measured and rewarded . . . what, exactly? Nothing important, I've discovered. Nothing sustaining. Just "aptitude."

That's why we're all here: we all showed aptitude. Aptitude for showing aptitude, mainly. That's what they wanted, so that's what we delivered. A talent for some things, a knack for many things, and a genius for one thing: running up the count.

Nobody told us it wouldn't be enough.

## chapter
# TWO

ACCORDING TO A PSYCHIATRIST I SAW DURING A LOW
spell in my early thirties, a person's education, his formal schooling, does little to shape his fate or personality compared to the
deeper, more mysterious process of his *development*. It's not what
we're taught that determines who we become, it's what we experience, he said, particularly in our earliest childhoods, before
conscious learning is even possible, when the self is a welter of
appetite and instinct and the world that surrounds it a sort of fog
out of which vivid, mythic figures emerge, sometimes offering
sustenance and comfort, sometimes delivering shocks and trau-
mas. The problem is that these events are largely lost to us, unlike the behaviors that they spawn, but he assured me that,
through skillful therapy and honest self-examination, people can
overcome, to some degree, the legacies of their buried pasts.

I agreed to give his theory a try. I spilled all my secrets, re-
counted all my dreams, and dredged up all my shames. We
talked masturbation, sibling rivalry, incest fantasies, sexual rejec-
tions, the death of a beloved childhood dog, the effects of a deep
depression my father suffered during my early teens that was

marked by frequent threats of suicide, my history with drugs and
alcohol, and a hundred other disturbing subjects that I should
have felt relieved to finally air. And yet we got nowhere. Nothing changed. I still couldn't sleep, keep a girlfriend, curb my
drinking, or pay my bills on time. But none of that was what
bothered me, finally. What bothered me was that I'd spent the
last ten months playing to my doctor's theories on developmen-
tal psychology rather than telling him what I believed to be the
simple truth about myself: that I was precisely the person I'd
been trained to be, and that the essence of my training was to
confuse the approval of my trainers—of whom he was just the
latest—with my own happiness.

"It sounds like you plan to quit therapy."

I nodded.

"A final observation?"

"Sure."

"Your feelings about authority figures remind me of your
descriptions of your father. You fear their power but also envy
it. You tend to ingratiate them initially, but then you despise
yourself for it and reject them, which is, in fact, a rejection of
yourself."

"I'll think about that. Thanks." I checked my watch. Eight
more minutes of this and I'd be free.

"One more thing," my doctor said. "A guess. You idolized
someone once. You had a hero. You saw in him an almost god-
like wisdom, a sort of benevolent omniscience. But then he
abandoned you—or you felt he did. Is that correct? Are we getting somewhere finally?"

I looked down at the floor, and then over at a wall—everywhere but at my doctor's face. Only moments ago I'd dismissed

him as a quack, but I'd misjudged him. I'd misjudged him badly. The man was a seer, a magician.

"Yes," I whispered.

"Describe him. Take your time."


**R**ear Admiral Robert Knox, Retired—Uncle Admiral, as I learned to call him—was my first teacher and my first love. I met him when I was four years old, in Fairfax, Virginia, near Washington, D.C., where my family was living in a small apartment building occupied mostly by people just out of college who were busy trying to get a start in life and by people on pensions who were just as busy keeping an eye on the younger people's children, who ran around in the grassy courtyard, unsupervised, throwing rocks and battling with sticks. I was one of the neglected runts. My father was studying patent law at night, clerking in a court during the day, and my mother was working part-time as a nurse and caring for my new baby brother, Andy. If I fell and skinned my knee, there was often no one to go crying to, but one day, after a scuffle with a bully that left me with a bloody nose, an old man who was reading in a lawn chair called me over, produced a handkerchief, twisted it into a point, and gently inserted it in my ruptured nostril.

When the bleeding stopped we went into his apartment, which was two doors down from ours, and he dabbed my face clean with a washcloth. Then he made us tea with milk and sugar, which he served with slices of Sara Lee pound cake. His movements were precise, efficient, tight, as though he was used to working in close quarters, and in no way did he evoke the fearsome strangers that my parents had warned me to beware of.

Indeed, he'd met my parents, he informed me, and he felt that it might ease their hectic lives if I were to let him watch me on occasion. He'd ask them about it. If they agreed, I should come over tomorrow morning at eight and we'd have our first "lesson."

"In what?"

"All sorts of things. I'll be in my study upstairs. Come right on up."

And so it began, my two-year private tutorial under a world-traveling old Scotsman who treated me not as a child but as a first mate. The vessel he'd helmed was named the *Pathfinder*. It belonged not to the U.S. Navy but to the Coast and Geodetic Survey, a little-known branch of the Treasury Department whose mission traced back to the time of President Jefferson, an era of far-flung cartographic quests. What Lewis and Clark were sent off to discover about the American continent's western wilderness, the corps of seagoing explorers that became the C&GS was tasked with learning about the coasts. Uncle Admiral's part in this endeavor ran from the twenties to the fifties and focused on the supremely crooked shorelines of Alaska and the Northwest.

"Name the chain," he asked me in his study, touching an index finger to his big globe.

"The Aleutians."

"That's correct. And from whom did we buy them? Which great nation?"

"Russia?"

He nodded, biting the woody stem of his dime-store corncob pipe. My pipe, identical, lay on his desk next to the mugs of milky chicory coffee he prepared for us each weekday morning at precisely eight hundred hours. Later, at twelve hundred hours on the dot, he'd whip up two bologna and mustard sandwiches. Then, exactly three hours later, he'd bring out the tea and pound cake. He lived as he had on shipboard in the Pacific: briskly, austerely, and by the clock. I found his routines reassuring and relaxing. At my parents' place, meals were served irregularly, squeezed in between other chores and obligations, and were frequently broken up by phone calls, but at Uncle Admiral's apartment routines ran smoothly, time never wobbled, and each bite was chewed and swallowed.

"Whose idea was the purchase of Alaska—a decision for which he was widely, harshly mocked?"

I didn't remember. I scanned the study for clues. A wooden slide rule resting on an atlas. A polished brass sextant in a felt-lined case. Shelf upon shelf of leather-bound photo albums documenting Uncle Admiral's meetings with everyone from a band of Inuit fishermen to the Queen of England. He stood the same way no matter who stood beside him, his arms at his sides and his shoulders squared, chin out. His uniform was an extraneous formality. His rectitude was intrinsic, skeletal.

"Secretary Seward," he said at last, sounding as if he'd known the fellow personally. For all I knew he might have. Cortés, Napoleon, and Edison, too. I was a bright child at four, and because of my daily drillings by my master (who'd served as an army sergeant in World War I) a prodigiously well-informed one who knew that nautical miles were longer than land miles, that the moon tugged the oceans across their floors. I could also read a little and use an abacus. What confused me, however, was Time and Mankind's place in it. How long had we dwelt on this planet? No idea. When had the monkey walking on all fours hauled itself upright and begun to speak? All I knew was that I'd just arrived here and that Uncle Admiral had preceded me, possibly by centuries. How long were centuries?

"Mankind" was a term my tutor used a lot, pronounced in the same familiar tone he brought to "Secretary Seward." The word marked him, I realized many years later while riding the train back to Princeton from D.C. after sharing with him what I knew would be our last-ever pot of chicory coffee, as a type I was being taught to view suspiciously: a patriarch. A patriarch first class. Soldier, sailor, surveyor, scholar, Scot. Guilty, guilty, guilty, guilty, guilty, guilty. At four, however, long before my fall into the bitter sophistication which allows us to disdain the figures who make our doubting—our very thinking—possible, I regarded Uncle Admiral as a chieftain and Mankind as the family we both belonged to. Mankind was all of us, everywhere and always, highest to lowest, first to last.

"This is a totem pole," he said, smoothing the page of a loose-leaf photo album. "I came across it in a Tlingit village while we were charting the waters around Sitka. The figures carved into it tell a tale in code. See the big bird on top? That's their raven god."

"Does it have powers?"

"They believe it does."

"But *does* it?"

"It may. For an Indian," he said.

I pressed him. "Only for an Indian?"

"I wouldn't presume to know."

At seventeen hundred hours, five p.m., we broke for what Uncle Admiral called "Happy Hour," which we enjoyed in the building's grassy courtyard, sitting on lawn chairs strung with nylon webbing. For him, a mint julep. For me, a lemonade.

Sometimes he brought out a wooden fruit crate that I could stand on while peering through his theodolite, an instrument of the surveyor's trade set on a tripod with telescoping legs.

"Choose a fixed point in the distance."

"I just see black."

"Pull back from the eyepiece."

"I see a flagpole now."

"Between you and the pole is a straight line slightly curved by the surface of the earth. The line runs due north. If you tracked it point to point, segment to segment, moving your theodolite, you'd end up in the dead center of the polar region."

"Where Santa Claus lives?"

Uncle Admiral said nothing, just cleaned his pipe. Fairy tales annoyed him, I was learning. His subject was Mankind. And earth, its home.

"The arctic is ice," I said.

"Ice and tundra. Yes."

"Tundra is frozen dirt?"

"Correct," he said.

"I wish I could walk on the tundra."

"You might someday."

"Maybe you'll come with me?"

"No," he said.

From one of the windows of his study we could see the Washington Monument. The obelisk was a giant survey stake. It marked a boundary beyond which lay the facts, the magnificent facts of totem poles and tribesmen, queens and coastlines, pyramids and Pygmies. Some of these facts, according to Uncle Admiral, were on display at the Smithsonian Institution, which he seemed to regard as America's true capital. The day we visited he took me to lunch at his club, the Cosmos Club, where men who shared his headwind-slicing posture ate chicken cutlets from heavy china, alternating their bites with sips of ice water. The exhibit I remember best used a system of colored lights to dramatize the behavior of gamma rays. It stayed with me because of Uncle Admiral's comment that "Solids, of course, aren't really solid." I asked to see the cursed Hope diamond afterward, which I'd heard about from my mother. He said, "Be serious." My nautical Socrates. Sometimes he was stern. What I learned from him, his master lesson—the one that would help me reconstitute my mind after it dissolved at Princeton, worn down by loneliness, drugs, and French philosophy—was that the world could indeed be grasped and navigated if one met it with a steady gaze. Matter wasn't truly solid, no, but it was packed tightly enough to set our feet upon.

One day Uncle Admiral opened a cardboard box and presented me with a sailor's cap whose eagle insignia and gold braid made it a near duplicate of his. As I tried it on he described to me the method by which he'd surveyed an inlet in Alaska. He'd tossed explosive charges overboard and used a sonar device to track the sound waves as they rippled toward the shore.

"Throwing bombs in the water. You're brave," I said.

"And, on at least one occasion, very stupid. I nearly lost half of my right arm." He rolled up his shirt sleeve to display the limb. There was no sign of damage that I could see, but I took the excuse to touch his skin. Its thinness alarmed me. I felt the bones beneath it.

The cap was a parting gift, I soon found out. A couple of days after it came, my parents began loading suitcases and trunks into the light-blue diesel Mercedes sedan which they'd bought used from Uncle Admiral, whose passion for German automobiles was his sole material indulgence. On the car's hood was a Rand McNally atlas opened to a map of the United States on which he'd shaded in a route that wiggled down from Washington to Georgia, where my father had taken a job at a small law firm that he'd leave after just a few months, as it turned out, in favor of the position at 3M. Uncle Admiral said he'd thought hard about our trip and chosen the route for a combination of reasons. It wasn't direct, he said, but it was scenic and passed through a number of towns and cities of great historical importance in what he called the "War Between the States."

"That's yours to keep," he said. He meant the atlas. Then he produced a ruler from a back pocket. "If you're wondering how far you are from something, lay the marked edge against the scale," he said. "But you know that already."

"Yes."

"Good boy," he said. "Be sure to visit London when you grow up."

"Why?"

"It's the greatest city in the world."

My father started the Mercedes. My mother, wiping at her eyes, climbed in the front as I squeezed into the back. I opened the atlas on my lap and kept it there all day and through the evening, across many rivers, over many bridges. I tried not to cry. I stayed busy with the ruler, tracking our progress in units of fifty miles. During one of our stops I left the cap behind on the counter of a diner but I didn't mention the loss when I discovered it. I felt stupid, confused, a new sensation for me. The farther I got from Uncle Admiral, the smaller and less capable I seemed to grow.

My psychiatrist, who'd encouraged these reminiscences and patiently listened to them for several sessions, fanning my hopes for a conclusive insight into my conflicted character, ended up profoundly disappointing me. He told me my memories weren't reliable. He said they amounted to a myth—of once having been the favorite of a great sage whose disappearance from my life had cast me into a world of fools—which was born, he said, of resentment toward my parents for turning their energies toward my little brother when I was most in need of affirmation. What's more, he said, I'd made of Uncle Admiral a fantasy figure of discipline and order that excused my failure, or unwillingness, to develop these qualities in myself or properly acknowledge them in others.

"Fair enough," I said. "Sounds good. Whatever." I knew I wouldn't be coming back to him. He'd made some good points but I sensed he made them often, to other patients besides me. Worse, I felt he'd insulted Uncle Admiral who, if he was a myth, had earned the privilege, just as I'd earned the privilege of keeping his myth intact. Everyone needs a personal creator, real or imagined, and he was mine. He'd shown me the world and where I stood in it and how it related to the places where others stood. He'd taught me to love learning for its own sake, as a way to feel less lost. Knowledge is power, people often say—and I later succumbed to this lie myself, regrettably—but Uncle Admiral, the mapmaker, knew better. Knowledge is a reckoning, he taught me, a way to assess your location, your true position, not a strategy for improving your position.

He steered me right, Uncle Admiral. He gave me the best start a four-year-old can get. But then I lost my bearings. I veered off course.

I went away to school.

# Chapter Three

MARINE, MINNESOTA, WHERE I ATTENDED GRADE SCHOOL, was a tidy bluff-top river town that belonged on a cake plate. The place seemed baked, not built. Its business district, centered around a park that featured a whitewashed wooden bandstand where actual barbershop quartets performed, consisted of a general store, a gas station, a hamburger restaurant, and a public library. Its people were mostly of Scandinavian heritage, meaning they didn't talk much but smiled constantly. Most had grown up there, or on nearby farms, but a few, like my family, had come from larger places where it was possible to witness a crime, contract an illness other than a cold, and attend a social gathering that wasn't a toddler's birthday party or a funeral for a ninety-five-year-old. The perfect place to raise a child, some felt.

But that wasn't why my father moved us there. He did it because the houses cost next to nothing and he could bow hunt in the nearby forests, fish in the river for smallmouth bass, and work in the yard in nothing but long underwear without being seen by his colleagues at 3M. He could also spit chewing tobacco on the sidewalk and go around covered in buck scent, wearing camouflage, with blood from the deer he'd just killed smeared on his hands. A Princeton man. Who knew? Not me. Not yet. Sometimes I wondered how my mother stood him. Though her formal higher education was limited to the Ohio State nursing program, she played the piano, kept art books on the coffee table, decorated the house with reproductions of posters by Toulouse-Lautrec, and occupied herself with novels by Dickens, Dreiser, and Conan Doyle while my father sat on the sofa next to her, cleaning his shotguns and watching college football.

Marine's elementary school was on a hill. It was the largest man-made structure in town, one of the newest, and by far the ugliest. Shape: rectangular. Material: beige brick. Constructed with tax money, it looked like tax money, a fiscal line item come to joyless life. Even the playground equipment seemed bureaucratic: a stainless-steel slide and a set of iron monkey bars on which one could picture army recruits glumly sweating their way through basic training. From the moment I entered the building's long tiled hallway, its colorless walls inadequately brightened with red-and-yellow construction-paper maple leaves, I wanted out. But out, I knew, meant through.

Because I'd already mastered my letters and numbers, I was free to ignore the lessons for a while and concentrate on the atmospherics. What hit me strongest were the smells. One of the nicest arose from the soft nests of twisty cedar pencil shavings in the tin sharpeners mounted on the walls. To please my earliest teachers, all middle-aged women, I dumped out the shavings in the wastebasket whenever I felt this nice gesture might be observed. My reward was gold foil stars, for "thoughtfulness." When I tired of appearing thoughtful, I sought out another, more thrilling odor: the brain-clearing fumes from jars of rubber cement. Education, intoxication, the link was forged.

I kept my wicked sniffing secret—I had a reputation to protect. Somehow I'd come to school with it: the good boy. The boy who let other students go first in line, who kept his lips from touching the water fountain, and who never asked to use the bathroom outside of designated breaks. When the teachers' felt erasers clogged up with chalk dust, I was the boy who carried them outside and pounded them clean against a wall, raising as much white powder as possible so I'd be coated in it when I returned. This entitled me to more gold stars as well as permission to wash up in the lavatory, where I could also relieve my pent-up bladder. There, I'd pump pink liquid soap into my palms, dry my skin with a rough brown paper towel, and reemerge with a new smell: bright-boy clean.

My favorite school odor those first few years belonged to a part-time music teacher, Ms. Hannah, a brown-eyed hippie girl with feather earrings and Navajo-like, lustrous dark hair. She wore, beneath her colorful loose clothes, a blend of plant oils that smelled like my idea of the tropical ports in Uncle Admiral's photos. Her job was to lead our third-grade music units. Everything was a "unit" at my school—or, in the later grades, a "module." The term evoked a machine part. It suggested that learning could be engineered, and that it had been, perhaps by government scientists—the same ones behind the Apollo program, maybe, about which we were constantly shown filmstrips. Our education, we got the sense, was related to matters of great national importance. It was part of an effort to keep America strong, most notably in the physical-fitness certificates that were personally signed by President Nixon, which I was still too young to compete for.

How music might aid this drive for global leadership I wasn't sure. Our first unit seemed frivolous. Ms. Hannah unpacked a carton of wooden blocks, called us forward, gave two blocks to each of us, then sent us back to the cockpit-style desks that reminded me of the belted seats on amusement rides at the state fair. "Today we're exploring rhythm," Ms. Hannah announced. She clapped together her own two blocks while chanting a series of notations chalked on the blackboard: "Ta Ta Ti-Ti Ta." Then she said, "Repeat." Once we mastered the sequence, she lengthened it. Then she lengthened it again. Finally, the unit ended—or so I thought. In fact, the rhythm unit never ended. It was pretty much all we did in music that year.

Our only breaks from this siege of syncopation came when Ms. Hannah brought out her guitar and sat on her desk with her legs crossed, revealing under her skirt a stack of silver ankle bracelets shaped like baby snakes, with ruby eyes. She produced the guitar without forewarning, apparently in response to strong emotions whose origins in her mysterious personal life were impossible for me to guess at but, to judge by the songs she chose, suggested deep gloom and disappointment. "*I've looked at love from both sides now*," she sang, "*From give and take, and still somehow / It's love's illusions I recall / I really don't know love at all.*" This was among her lighter numbers. Most of them were unsettling, even shocking. One song, from the movie *Billy Jack*, the story of a half-breed Indian who murdered people who threatened the environment, ended with the terrifying lyrics "*There won't be any trumpets blowing / Come the judgment day / On the bloody morning after* / *One tin soldier rides away.*" The song that spooked me most, though, was by the Beatles: "*wearing the face that she keeps in a jar by the door* / *All the lonely people* / *Where do they all come from?*"

From wherever Ms. Hannah dwelt, I came to feel, because in the weeks that followed Valentine's Day, after the cupids came down in the classrooms and the rabbits and chicks went up, she sunk even further into her dim blue world. Her voice grew croaky, husky, soft, and her playlist dwindled to "The Circle Game" and "Send in the Clowns." Beneath the layer of floral essences which distinguished her from the other teachers—old ladies who reeked of witch hazel and baby powder—I thought I detected a sharper odor: despair.

"Ms. Hannah?" I said one morning.

"What is it, Walter?" We were alone, the unit over. My classmates were all outside at recess celebrating an April warm spell with a muddy game of kickball.

"You seem so sad these days," I said.

"I can't say I'm very happy about our world right now."

Ms. Hannah laid her guitar in a black case whose satin lining was covered with decals. There were rainbows, peace signs, doves, and a chain of stick-figure children holding hands. I gathered that they were symbols of her hope for a gentler, kinder era. She'd told our class many times that music "healed" and had even asserted that it might end the war someday, if the politicians would just wake up. I took this to mean that politicians didn't listen to much music for some reason, or at least not to the kind Ms. Hannah played. I couldn't blame them. It was depressing, and they had jobs to do.

"Well, I hope you feel better," I said. I had a crush on her.

"That's hard when young men are dying for no good reason, but I promise you I'll try." She closed the guitar case, latched it, gripped its handle, and looked past me toward the door. She had other units to teach at other schools, which made me jealous when I thought about it. I feared she had a favorite student somewhere. A boy, perhaps, who wasn't at all like me. Someone more concerned with peace.

As she was about to go, she touched my shoulder. "Maybe I have been a little down," she said. "Human beings have rhythms, too, you know. You've heard the expression: 'The rhythms of the heart'?"

I nodded as though I had.

"That's all it is. It's nothing more than that."

"Have I ever told you how nice you smell?" I said.

"No, but I'm glad you feel that way. You're sweet."

"You're welcome," I said.

"You made my day."

She kissed me on the hair and brushed past me out the door. A few minutes later, on the playground swing set, I reached the high point in one of my long arcs and felt the chains momentarily go slack. I could see out to the street in front of the school, where Ms. Hannah was getting into the brown van of the young man who sometimes picked her up and who, I suddenly knew, had hurt her somehow. The van stayed parked for a while, then rumbled off, and I realized I'd just learned something important—not about music, about teachers. They were people. Lonely people, often, who weren't really free to share their lives with us but longed for appreciation, just as I did. And why not give it to them now and then? Maybe they would give it back to me.

Certain questions which grown-ups deem unanswerable begin as answers which children find unquestionable. For example: what is Death? To me at eight years old, death was the signal for a person's loved ones to cry and look stricken for a while and then begin dividing up his stuff. What is Beauty? The thing that made me like things when nobody was pushing me to like them. And what is Art? In third grade, I felt I knew. An artwork was any useless, random object created in order to break up the school day and then toted home to show off to one's parents, after which it was misplaced or thrown away.

The art units at my elementary school were even emptier than the music units. They were like recess periods held indoors. Art, the way my teachers introduced it, wasn't really a subject, as math and science were, but a state of mind. Achieving this state required glue and scissors, sometimes glitter, occasionally bits of yarn, and long stretches of silence. Art was a form of stillness, dull and peaceful, and yet we were urged to approach it with great excitement, as though enduring boredom and immobility liberated what was best in people.

"What's *that* thing?" my father asked me one afternoon. It was November, well into the school year, and my art teacher was pushing a new line: that art, to be good, should show *emotion*. This contradicted her old line: that art was good no matter what.

"It started out," I said, "as a triceratops charging a stegosaurus that you can't see except for the tip of its snout there at the edge, under the boulders shooting from the volcano."

"So how come it didn't stay all that?"

"My teacher."

"What about her?"

"She told me to open up."

"Open up in what respect?"

"By drawing forms instead of objects."

"The distinction there being . . . ?"

"All I know," I said, "is what she told me. It's fine that I draw good dinosaurs, she said, but drawing things that look like other things—things that we have pictures of already—isn't really art, it's copying. Art is feelings. She wants me to draw feelings. That's what those squiggles are. Those wavy parts."

My father nodded. Then he went hunting. In a pipe in the wall I could hear the water draining from my mother's bath upstairs. To spare her the awkwardness and insincerity of having to show pride in my botched picture, I crumpled it up and stuffed it in my corduroys, where it stayed hidden until laundry day.

"What's this?" my mother said.

"Some art I made."

"I love it."

"Why?"

"It's different."

"Than what?" I said.

"Than what you usually do. There's something new here."

"Feelings."

"Is that it? Huh. I think you're right."

That's when, art-wise, I became a fraud. With the pure, uncorrupted logic which God grants eight-year-olds, I reasoned that if art was made of feelings and feelings were secret, known only to the artist, then art could be anything you said it was. Collage by collage, tempera by tempera, I practiced producing mysterious oddities to which I could attach invented feelings. My stories about my art *became* my art. "This decoupage is about how sad I get when my father leaves on a long business trip." "This watercolor shows my happiness when it snows and I can use my sled." These stories brought praise and sometimes hugs, eventually convincing me that art was about one feeling above all others: being loved. Or wanting to be loved. And once I discovered this, I got straight As.

**A** rope dangled from the ceiling of the gymnasium. If we could climb it fast enough and high enough, we'd be eligible for a framed certificate signed by our nation's commander in chief— a man of humble beginnings, my father told me, who'd worked his way through law school, entered politics, suffered much ridicule from "egghead" types who lived in "ivory towers," and finally prevailed by "giving them the finger." You could think what you want about Nixon, my father said, but the man was no quitter, he had grit, and no one had ever given him anything; he'd taken what he had by force of will. No wonder I wanted so badly to climb that rope for him and bring home his autograph to show my father.

I hung back and let my friends go first. They attacked the rope with zeal, gaining their first few feet through sheer momentum, but for most of them there came a point when it was clear they'd rise no farther no matter how desperately they strained. The other kids would crowd in under them and holler encouragement, but all this accomplished was to rob the climbers of a dignified glide back to the floor. Instead, they were forced to put on a futile show, to claw and grunt and slip back even farther, turning what might have been a quick defeat into a protracted humiliation.

I panicked when my turn came. I'd already disappointed the president in two less-strenuous events—chin-ups and the standing broad jump—and another defeat, I feared, would crush me utterly and show me up as a poor citizen. It would prove that I wasn't just weak but flawed, defective, and likely to prove a burden on my country should it ever be put to some great test such as resisting a foreign invasion. As I understood the program, the highly specific performance standards required to earn the fitness certificate reflected desirable or normal levels of strength, agility, and speed for healthy young American males. How these levels had been determined I wasn't certain—by NASA or the Marine Corps, possibly—but I did understand that falling short of them was not a purely private matter.

I gripped the rope with clammy palms. The gym teacher blew his whistle and clicked his stopwatch. Five feet, six feet, six feet and an inch. I was already flagging and couldn't hide it, certainly not from myself or from my observant classmates, who, I saw when I looked down, had already started massing for their death cheer. I felt puny, crippled, trapped. This wasn't art or music, this was gym, and quick-wittedness couldn't help me here. I was up against gravity, which can't be fooled, and the implacable limits of my physique, which my father had urged me to strengthen through calisthenics but hadn't bothered to demonstrate which ones.

"Go! Don't quit! You can make it! Reach!" they cried.

I locked my ankles around the rope. My slide began. I checked it by clenching my thighs, slid farther, groaned, and imagined the president shaking hands with a line of strapping boys who would someday bring glory to America, in war, perhaps, or by building a base on Mars, while I lay feebly on a couch, watching their exploits on TV. Then, for the first time since I'd entered school, I yielded, I folded, I gave up. I landed on the gym mat, found my feet, and as the next aspirant approached the rope, I wished him luck, sincerely, without envy. People were different. Some smart, some strong. The boy scrambled upward, on track to reach the ceiling, and I found myself pitying him, oddly, because I knew his triumph would be brief, his moment of conquest would be over soon, while mine, which would be of another sort—mental, not physical; fate had spoken—would only build and build.

Could Nixon have climbed that rope? I doubted it. But he could make others climb it, and that was true strength. The strength I wanted for myself.

In fourth grade I learned that reading was serious business, not just a pleasant way to pass the time, and that like medicine or engineering, it had a definite, valuable purpose: to foster "comprehension." I learned this from boxes of plastic quiz cards whose labels bore the letters SRA. The letters stood for Science Research Associates, which was identified somewhere on the boxes as a division of IBM, the giant computer firm whose amazing machines, I gathered from the news, were crucial in the sophisticated activities which underlay our modern way of life, from weather forecasting to missile guidance. That IBM had taken on the job of providing the nation's grade schools with color-coded essay cards arranged by steadily increasing difficulty and capable, according to the teacher, of enriching and assessing students' "language capabilities" suggested to me, once again, that I was part of a vast and vital program, success in which would confer colossal rewards, possibly even widespread public gratitude.

The structure of the SRA kits encouraged scorekeeping and competition. Toward the middle of the second quarter, having finished the blue cards and plunged into the green, I consulted a homemade tally sheet taped to the bottom of my desk's hinged lid and determined that, comprehension-wise, I was a solid week ahead of my two closest rivals: Brian Dahl, of whose background I knew little, and Karla Miller, the child of farmers who cultivated a modest patch of swampy acreage. The sheet was a secret and, I thought, unique, but later that month evidence emerged that Karla was keeping a similar log.

"I did some math," she said. "By Friday I'll be one card back from Brian, but by the end of next Monday I'll be past him. Then it'll be just you and me."

I showed no reaction, which took great effort. To behold one's least noble traits in someone else, and in a refined and concentrated form, is a piercing, destabilizing experience.

"It's not like I want to prove I'm better," said Karla. "I just think it makes it more fun if it's a contest. You look mad at me."

"No, I don't," I said.

Because we'd been forced from our desks by the custodian, who'd set up a ladder in our row to hunt for a leak that had warped some ceiling tiles, Karla and I were sitting on the floor, our SRA kits open on our laps, our bodies positioned hip to hip but at an angle to give us privacy. When she piped up about her game plan, I was extracting a fresh card from my kit. My reflex was to push the card back down so as to hide its number and color, but I thought better of the move. If observed, it might make me seem uncertain, and Karla might try to play on my anxiety.

A war of nerves ensued. I wasn't prepared for it. If I'd given some thought to Karla's situation as the poorest kid in class but also one of the cleverest, I might have expected such a challenge, but the problem was that I, like most of us, rarely thought about Karla much at all. Why should we? Her clothes were drab, her skin was dull, and her habit of responding with a vague chuckle to virtually anything anyone said to her—greeting, insult, request, or knock-knock joke—made it impossible to gauge her moods. I barely knew her, I realized, but I was starting to. She was like me, but slyer, more calculating, and whatever she said about "fun," I strongly sensed that she wouldn't be gracious in victory but vicious. This year, next year, and all the way through school.

I vowed to stick to my program, to stay calm. I set my SRA card on my knee and skimmed a couple of paragraphs on icebergs, ignoring three-quarters of the text in order to focus on the dates and numbers, the quotations and proper nouns, which usually formed the answers to the questions printed underneath the essays. This process involved neither reading nor comprehension; it was more like sifting sand for seashells. Karla seemed not to notice. I peeked at the card on the floor in front of her—its topic was bird migration—but I couldn't remember any of its points despite having read it only days before.

The contest intensified but I stayed cool, convinced that I had a natural mental edge. Color by color, with Karla at my back, I acquainted myself with the world that IBM seemed to deem most deserving of comprehension. It was a world of technology and optimism, of aviation and antibiotics. Research submarines scoured its deepest oceans for valuable mineral deposits. Radar dishes in the arctic guarded the North American continent from sneak attacks by enemy bombers. The world was steadily improving. The descendants of slaves were attending top colleges. Women were taking seats in Congress. Birds that were thought to be extinct had been spotted mating in the wild. There were problems, too, of course—smog and drug abuse and cancer—but the essays implied that they'd be solved soon.

The race began to tighten. Karla passed Brian, just as she'd predicted. He rallied and almost caught up to her, but then slipped back a few days later. He didn't seem to care. He read for the reasons I only pretended to read—for understanding, out of actual interest—and sometimes he looked up from his cards as though he were truly reflecting on their contents.

Once the race had narrowed to Karla and me, I tried to move more swiftly through the cards by reading the questions at the bottom first and circling back to the essays to find the answers. This trick worked so well that I wondered if IBM was really the marvel people said it was. From January until the grass turned green, I stayed a full color ahead of Karla, who seemed baffled by my continued lead and finally resorted to a dirty trick.

"Walter," she said to me, pointing at her card, "I'm having a little trouble with this word. What's 'radiate'?"

"You should use your pocket dictionary."

"The print's too small and my glasses haven't come yet. I just had an eye exam. I didn't do well. It's why I've been getting headaches, the doctor said."

I didn't believe her, but the damage was done: I lost my ability to concentrate. An essay on coral reefs that I should have completed in ten minutes took me almost twenty, mostly because I kept glancing over at Karla, who was playing her blind act to the hilt, holding her card at a distance from her face, squinting, then bringing it closer, then moving it back again. I couldn't help thinking it was a masquerade arising from some intense determination that exceeded even my own.

I decided to be gallant. I slowed my pace, but by degrees, forcing Karla to struggle to surpass me and granting her a seemingly honest victory. As I'd expected, she gloated afterward, not out loud but in her manner, affecting a strut when she passed me in the hallway and habitually raising her hand in class whenever I raised mine. But I gloated, too—for my chivalrous refusal to dispel her illusion of superiority. What a prince I'd been, I thought, and how noble to bow before those one might have vanquished.

But then something happened that knocked me off my perch. As we cleaned out our desks a few days before vacation, filling the wastebaskets with pencil stubs and plugged-up bottles of Elmer's glue, Karla appeared in the aisle beside me holding out a small pink plastic case.

"My glasses came," she said. "You want to see?"

She settled the frames on the thin bridge of her nose and gazed at me through a pair of lenses whose formidable thickness and convexity spoke strongly of optical necessity. A prickly flush spread up my neck; the girl was a visual cripple, she'd told the truth, and the fortitude it must have taken to grapple with the SRA cards was painful to consider, as was the margin by which she would have bested me if she'd had the glasses all along. She knew this, too. She had to. Who'd spared whom? She was a queen, this girl. Moral royalty.

But then she had to rub it in by telling me what I was, which I didn't appreciate at all. It didn't decrease my respect for her—it raised it—but it did guarantee I'd avoid her from then on.

"Students who read the questions first are only cheating themselves," she said. "I'm glad I'm not you. I really am. When I realized what you were doing, it ticked me off at first, but then I decided to pray for you instead. It softened my heart. I'm really glad I did it. I just wish you'd pray for yourself sometimes. You need to."

I wasn't sure what a person should say to this, or if he could be expected to say anything.

"Well, have a fantastic summer," Karla said.

"You, too," I mumbled. She smiled and turned to go. I was struck by an impulse to stop her and apologize—our talk seemed emotionally incomplete somehow—but I wasn't certain what I was sorry for, because I hadn't harmed her, it turned out, and the harm that she seemed to feel I'd done myself (finding an angle, and then playing it) wasn't within my power to give up.

Chapter
**Four**

---

MIDWESTERN COUNTRY SUMMERS, ALL ALIKE, BROAD GREEN immensities of humid tedium, nothing to do but wade barefoot in the river, nowhere to go but to the store for Popsicles, no one to talk to but the dog. By July, I stopped heeding the shrill tornado sirens and couldn't be bothered to slap the fat mosquitoes drilling my neck behind my ears. There were pickles and mayonnaise on every sandwich, a dying wasp in every cup of Kool-Aid. I built a model rocket. It failed in flight. I sent away for a slingshot. It never came. On weekends, I went fishing with my father, hypnotized by the ripples around my bobber, and in the firefly evenings after supper I pitched rocks into the trees just to hear them go ripping through the leaves. I sat on a stump with a *Playboy* from a trash bin, rehearsing the party jokes, relishing the nipples. There was always the library, my mother said, and she brought me there at every excuse, but the books were in poor condition, missing pages, and the best ones, like *A Wrinkle in Time* and the Hardy Boys series, seemed to be permanently checked out. Instead I ran off to the woods to break an arm or sped away on my bike to gash a shin. In August there was always a week in bed, a stretch of seclusion, Tylenol and root beer. There was always a murder on my AM radio, a shouting match in my parents' bedroom, a grandparent dozing on our sofa. And then it was over. Time to buy new shoes. Time to start school again, to wake back up, with nothing to show for the summer but a fresh haircut and a bird skull I'd found in a puddle. But nothing learned.

**M**ath had always been a cinch for me. My teachers said I had a head for numbers. But then, in fifth grade, math turned into something else. Letters were added. Symbols. Diagrams. "Problems" that had once had "answers" became "equations" with "solutions." Mysteries emerged. The value of pi, we learned, could only be estimated, and we were informed that it was possible to count backward from zero, not just forward from one. I kept up with these puzzles, but I didn't like them; they seemed to be pointing toward a realm of darkness, toward a less reliable reality.

It didn't help that Marine was changing, too. The town's adults, including my mother and father, were throwing more parties than in years past, and the parties were running later into the nights. My brother and I could feel them roaring beneath us as we lay in our beds watching talk shows from Los Angeles whose naughty banter and eccentric guests—a willowy hippie who strummed a ukulele, a bearded fat man who performed bad card tricks, a Spanish bombshell in a sequined sheath who shimmied her hips and yodeled nonsense—seemed to echo the strange vibrations we'd been feeling for a while by then. The first shock came when Marine's new Lutheran pastor showed up for services one Sunday morning driving a motorcycle with a chrome gas tank and a suntanned girlfriend on the back. Soon afterward, someone set fire to the bandstand and spray-painted peace signs on the general store. Then the elm trees started dying, whole majestic arching columns of them, the cores of their trunks chewed to sawdust by foreign beetles. This blight coincided with the news that the parents of three of my best friends, three separate couples, were filing for divorces, and that one of the wives planned to marry one of the husbands. But the most jolting development, to my mind, was the appearance of a bumper sticker on two of my mother's best friends' station wagons: BAN THE BRA! Was it a joke? The slogan seemed ominously juvenile. Our parents, I began to fear, were no longer in any condition to protect us.

School was no refuge. The math units disturbed me, and Mr. Applebaum, our fifth-grade teacher, who was younger than the others, made me jumpy. His manner was boyish and exuberant, but there was a savagery to his vitality, especially on the subject of Vietnam. He supported the war. He loved it, actually, and those who didn't love it disgusted him. He called them names. They were sissies, perverts, traitors. To counter the damage he said that they were doing to our national morale, he had each of us write a letter to a soldier. To fire us up, he described the distant GIs as noble giants beset by tricky peasants too cowardly to fight them man-to-man. Instead, the fiends used booby traps that fired poisoned shrapnel through our guys' feet or snared their boots in coiled vines and snatched their bodies up into the treetops. The letter I wrote after hearing about these horrors was short and lazy. I assumed that the soldier it was addressed to would be dead by the time that it arrived.

Because it allowed him to talk about the war and other topics he found infuriating, Mr. Applebaum's favorite subject was social studies. At first the units were textbook-based, but later he dismissed the books as biased and adopted an informal approach using stories from the news. He emphasized student riots, gun control, and violent crimes committed by drug abusers, coming always to the same conclusions: American men were becoming "soft old ladies," young people weren't getting enough exercise, and no one knew the value of money. When he stopped ranting, he asked for our opinions, urging us to argue with him, but we knew better than to comply. We confined ourselves to asking questions formulated to inspire fresh diatribes. Most of these questions were asked by me, since few of my classmates followed current events and knew just which subjects (the Arabs, ecology, acid rock, Jane Fonda) were most likely to arouse him.

In return for playing to his obsessions, I expected good grades from Mr. Applebaum. I got them. But I didn't quite win him over. On the comment line of my first-quarter report card, and again in a parent-teacher conference, he remarked negatively on my "adjustment" and the quality of my "detail work." I felt betrayed. I also felt exposed. The charges seemed vague to me but also justified, pointing to a weakness in my makeup that I'd grown increasingly aware of. Something was missing in me. Some central element. Not intelligence but whatever guides intelligence. Self-discipline? I wasn't sure. What stung was that someone as nutty as Mr. Applebaum could see into me at all. I feared this meant that I was crazy, too.

In February, the man got worse. He became obsessed with Wounded Knee, a violent confrontation in South Dakota between a group of radical Indians and a squad of FBI men backed by armored vehicles and helicopters. Our social-studies units turned into updates about the developing situation. Shots fired from inside the compound. Fire returned from the perimeter. No casualties among the lawmen, an unknown number of wounded among the Sioux. As Mr. Applebaum described him, the Indians' leader, Russell Means, was a threat to the Constitution, whatever that meant, as well as a secret ally of Russia. Photos of Means were passed around the class, presumably so we could focus our revulsion and maybe so we could spot him in a crowd should the Pine Ridge rebels break the cordon. Mr. Applebaum took this possibility seriously, and he encouraged us to do the same. South Dakota bordered Minnesota, also the home to many Indians.

"This thing might go national," he said one day.

When there was no news from the front, Mr. Applebaum strove to place the crisis in a wider, historical perspective. The Indians, he told us, were a proud, resourceful people who'd ruled the Great Plains from before the days of firearms, but when the white man entered the scene with his forged metal tools, conflict between the groups became inevitable. War was to history, he said, what rain was to a garden. Without it, society would wither. He praised the Indian fighters for their fierce spirit, but he lambasted them for not accepting defeat. America's tribes, he let us know, had never formally, legally surrendered. Having retreated to their reservations, they were still plotting a final campaign.

"We have tanks, though," a kid beside me said.

"But will we use them? Do we have the will?" Mr. Applebaum turned to me, his telepath. "Explain to Brian why today's Americans don't have the guts to use tanks on Indians."

"We don't work hard or get enough fresh air."

My complicity in these dialogues left me feeling dirty when the bell rang. Eager to breathe fresh air myself, I asked my father to take me fishing one evening, a few days after the season opener. The frosty stone steps from our house down to the river demanded careful footwork as I followed him to our fiberglass boat. We hadn't used it since last summer and it had deteriorated, like everything. My friends' parents' divorces were final now, the elms along Judd Street were mostly gone, and the bumper-sticker plague had worsened, its slogans having grown blunter and more jolting (BACK OFF, ASSHOLE; STICK IT, TRICKY DICKY!). No one went near the bandstand anymore because of a hypodermic needle that had been found in the grass beside its steps.

My father and I didn't say much on the river. We tried all our lures, from a silver-bellied Rapala to a rubber-skirted Hula Popper, but didn't attract any strikes. I didn't care. I liked staring at the moving water. It beat imagining letters to dead soldiers soaking up rain on the floors of Asian jungles. It beat hearing Mr. Applebaum describe the role of LSD and devil worship in a recent California murder.

My father cast his Hula Popper. "How's school?"

"The same, pretty much. I'm doing fine."

"Comfortable yet with algebra?"

"Adjusting."

"How about that lunatic young teacher?"

I grinned. I hadn't realized my father knew.

"All he talks about is Wounded Knee."

My father cast his lure again. I didn't know which side he'd taken in the battle with the Indians. The government's, probably. He voted Republican. Then again, he'd grown a mustache last fall and let his sideburns creep longer and go all bushy.

"What does Applebaum think?" he asked me.

"Shoot them. They never surrendered. Make them pay."

My father fell silent, reeling in his lure. It spluttered noisily along the surface, meant to imitate a crippled minnow. The effect drove bass crazy, supposedly. Not tonight, though.

"They're Americans, too," my father finally said. I waited for him to say more, but that was it.

He yanked the cord on our Johnson outboard motor and headed down the river, away from town, toward the maze of sloughs we called Rice Lake. We'd be out for at least another two hours, this meant, in jackets too thin for the chill of springtime dusk, but I wasn't ready to go back. The water seemed safer than the land these days.

The Indians dropped their weapons soon after that and Mr. Applebaum wheeled in a TV set so we could enjoy the scenes of their surrender. Heads down, in handcuffs, lines of captives shuffled toward armored wagons, guarded by FBI agents with rifles. Mr. Applebaum paced the aisles between our desks and made a fist as the wagons rolled away, pulling dust clouds behind them down a straight dirt road.

"Walter, tell us something."

I didn't look up.

"Why is our nation safer and better off—socially, constitutionally, in all ways—than it was at this time yesterday?"

"I don't know," I said.

"Oh, please. Come on."

But I couldn't do it, not this time. I was through, and my social-studies grade reflected it when I received my report card a month later. I didn't mind for once. I didn't care. I could afford this slipup, I decided, because there would probably never be another one. I wasn't brave. I just happened to be tired.

# Chapter Five

To OUR PARENTS, WHO JUDGED PEOPLE BY THEIR ACTIONS rather than their looks, Mr. Hulbertson was a good man, a doer of many civic-minded deeds, but to us, his sixth-grade students, whose senses remained unclouded by notions of virtue, he was an ugly man with noxious breath. But that was just our first impression. As the school year went on and contact displaced impact, a few of us, and eventually a lot of us, revised our view of him. He wasn't ugly, he was loathsome. With his mouthful of stumpy, charred-looking gray teeth and his mildewed rag of lank black beard, he was abominable on every level, and what we'd initially thought of as his "bad breath" was neither *his,* we discovered, nor truly *breath*, since it stank not only on the ex-hale but slightly prior to the inhale, when a breath isn't even a breath yet, only air.

"Forget about algebra today. It's time we discussed something real," he told the class a month or two into the year. He put down the chalk stick he'd been using, grabbed an eraser, and wiped the blackboard clean with an abrupt and aggressive Z-shaped stroke that loosed flecks of gray dandruff from his beard.

"Those of you who read the paper," he said, "may have gotten wind of this already. The rest of you, I'll catch you up. Just recently, in one of our large cities, a handsome, healthy, athletic adult man decided that he'd prefer to be a female."

Mr. Hulbertson gave us time for questions then, but he was being premature since no one yet knew what he was talking about. When no questions were asked, he located his only stick of chalk that wasn't a splintered, snapped-off stub (he bore down like crazy when he used the stuff) and sketched on the board an enormous drooping curve that looked like a wind sock when there's no wind.

"I can make this whole business much clearer with a story. Sometimes a man at a restaurant or a bar will excuse himself to empty his bladder. He'll go to the restroom. He'll stand over a urinal. He'll guide his penis through his open fly (let's be mature today; not his *thing*, his *penis*) and as he's holding it and aiming his urine stream, he'll look down and think: this doesn't feel like *mine*. Sometimes I wish I didn't even *have* it. Sometimes I wish a surgeon could just *remove* it and give me something else that feels more . . . natural."

I can't describe the class's reaction because I was so absorbed in mine, which was to find myself wondering—*intensely*, after a lifetime of barely caring—if my Levi's were securely zipped.

Mr. Hulbertson reached out with his chalk and slashed a bold X through his penis diagram. He'd turned it from a drawing into a diagram by labeling it "Adult Male Genitalia."

"The man wants to be a woman—he's made his mind up. No more acting. No more masquerading. If he has to, he'll do the surgery *himself*."

Shockingly, a hand went up. It appeared at the far edge of

my vision, and all I could see was the motion, not who made it. "He'd need to sterilize his knife and have a first aid kit with lots of gauze and iodine. He'd want a tube of sunburn cream for pain, but only if it was sterile and brand-new." The voice, it turned out, belonged to Jenny Johnson, who'd been campaigning for teacher's pet that year.

"I'm grateful. I thank you, Jenny," the monster said. His policy was to thank her for speaking up, pretty much no matter what she said, as a way of reproaching the rest of us for cowering at our desks. "At this point in history, fortunately," he said, "such risky procedures aren't necessary. Specialists can perform the operation in a modern hospital environment."

More time was bestowed on us for questions. None came. Our teacher sighed, a thin expulsion of vapor which, if it hit your face, could make your eyes sting. He shook his bulb-shaped, itchy-looking head, erased the penis diagram, and carved a fresh equation into the blackboard, the tip of his chalk stick crumbling from the pressure.

Then, without pausing, he erased the numbers.

"Screw it—I'm not in the mood for math today. Independent reading time," he said. "I'm getting coffee in the lounge."

Once his absence had lasted a few minutes and had begun to feel dependable, a kid named Warren said, "He dreamed that up."

"How would you know?" a kid beside me asked him.

"Think about it. Use some common sense. There's doctors who'll cut off your cock if you just *ask*?"

The discussion ended there. Afterward, I pretended it hadn't occurred. Then a week later, while standing in the lunch line, I got a whiff of sour, beard-stained air and felt a limp arm being laid across my shoulders. It was a left arm with a dangling hand that brushed against the breast pocket of my shirt, then inched its way between the top two buttons, across the skin of my bare chest, and tweaked my left nipple with two chapped fingertips.

"Does that feel nice?"

"Mr. Hulbertson!"

He fled.

But he came back. When we returned to school the following morning, there he was again, standing by the door, taking attendance on a clipboard with streaks of what looked like egg yolk in his beard. It appeared there was no God. This left only our parents to protect us. A troubling thought. Our parents adored the man.

Ever since kindergarten, school and home had been very different places, but during my first semester with Mr. Hulbertson they became *opposite* places, mirror worlds. Sometimes at dinner I'd watch my father eat while my left nipple, which had never recovered, prickled and tingled beneath my shirt. How could he just sit there cutting his steak? How could my mother just stand there boiling broccoli? How did they manage to carry on at all without somehow sensing that their oldest son had spent his day imprisoned in a classroom with someone whose hands roamed under students' clothes?

"Has he chosen a play yet?" my mother asked me.

"It's between *My Fair Lady* and *Tom Sawyer.*"

My mother was referring to Mr. Hulbertson's annual sixth-grade musical comedy, a beloved institution in Marine. Its rehearsal and production took several months, during which normal schoolwork was suspended. The play was supposed to represent a treat for kids, a kind of grade-school graduation present. It was also considered a gift to the community, due to its lavish, semiprofessional scale. *Oliver!*, last year's show, had been a hit, running for three straight sold-out nights at the historic auditorium inside Marine's pioneer-era town hall. My family, like most families in town, attended all three shows to help recoup the cost of the spectacular. Those had been grueling, restless nights for me, tinged by a dread of the fraudulent hysteria that broke out every few minutes in the hall. Whenever someone's rouged-up son or daughter missed a note or flubbed a line, the crowd would burst forth with crashing gaiety, stomping their feet and slapping their neighbors' backs, while Mr. Hulbertson, visible in the wings, pantomimed a look of pained perfectionism and dabbed at his forehead with a handkerchief.

"No contest," my father said. "He'll choose *Tom Sawyer*. We're thirty miles from the Mississippi here, same basic landscape, almost the same town."

"The same as what?" I asked.

My father looked at my mother. She read, he didn't. "That place in Missouri, Millie."

"Hannibal."

"Interesting. Rhymes with 'cannibal,'" I said. I was giving them a clue. I didn't expect them to understand its meaning, but I wanted to get it out there in case something terrible happened later on.

After announcing the play would be *Tom Sawyer*, Mr. Hulbertson held tryouts for its two main roles.

"Toms should line up over here," he told the class, "and all of you panting, blushing little Beckys should gather up close here to my left."

An hour-long kissing competition ensued. Mr. Hulbertson called each boy to stand in front of him and had the girls step forward one by one to let the boy embrace them and to embrace him back. Through a humiliating process of personalized coaching ("Greg, lean in more," "Diane, relax your torso," "Brian, let's have you stick that handsome chest out," "Open your mouth, Kim, you're not a snapping turtle!"), the six potential Tom-and-Becky pairs which Mr. Hulbertson deemed most "convincing" were isolated from the rest. None of the duos made sense to me. Two were composed of well-known enemies, one involved a freakish fat-and-thin match, and the other three seemed to be cruel experiments in emotional incompatibility.

Bitter scenes arose as the six couples were winnowed to a final three. Two of the Toms fell into a scuffle after having to swap their Beckys. When the fat Becky learned she wouldn't make the cut because her kissing style, as Mr. Hulbertson said, was "hesitant and indirect," she crossed her arms and sat down on the floor and vowed not to budge until he changed his mind. Moments later, Leslie, the class beauty, wrested herself from the arms of the delinquent whose filthy mouth she'd been urged to stick her tongue in and ran off bawling to the lavatory. Sarah, her overdeveloped, shy best friend, who remained in competition (paired with lucky me), was dispatched by our lecherous teacher to coax poor Leslie back into the torture chamber. When Sarah returned, she said Leslie wanted to talk to Paula, whom our teacher had matched with Brian, the schoolyard dreamboat, whom Leslie had a well-known crush on. Mr. Hulbertson said to Paula as she left: "Tell that brat to drag her sweet ass back here and get with the fucking program. No more crap."

As we waited for the mission to play out, Mr. Hulbertson gazed out the window in the fashion of an irritable genius let down by a world of silly dullards. When Sarah returned—alone, no Paula—he turned on his heels like an army officer and marched into the hall, trailed by everyone but Edward, a detached Jehovah's Witness. We gathered at the girls' room door, whose customary guarantee of privacy our teacher chose to respect, amazingly. He knocked on it, he spoke loud words through it, but he didn't touch its knob, even when a fight broke out behind it that was audible all through the hall. Paper towels went screaming off their racks, curses were hurled, a trash can banged a wall, and Leslie screamed, "Brian's mine, you little witch!"

As everybody was bunching up to listen, I chanced to glance down and see my teacher's right hand plunged into a front pocket of Sarah's jeans. The hand wasn't still; it was grabbing around down there, stretching and distorting the tight denim. I lifted my gaze to Sarah's face, which seemed to be in the process of disappearing. Her eyes, squeezed shut, were little wrinkled patches, her cheeks were skin stuck flat to bone, and her nose had shriveled into a pink bump.

The door to the girls' room opened and the Beckys stepped forth as if nothing had happened, like perfect friends, though Leslie was pressing a bloodstained clump of toilet paper tight against her nostrils. Mr. Hulbertson spread his arms. They let him hug them. They walked back to the classroom as a trio. Then the kissing tournament resumed. I was cut in the end, demoted from Tom to Huck, but I knew by then a lead role would probably require many hours of special rehearsal alone with the director, and I wasn't disappointed.

Two decades later, the night before the funeral, my mother sat in her kitchen and described to me Mr. Hulbertson's last day as a teacher. Responding to a complaint filed by a female student's mother, a deputy sheriff showed up in his classroom and asked him into the hallway for a chat. When he returned, he crossed behind his desk to one of the tall windows that faced the playground, heaved it open, vaulted over the sill, and took off running past the jungle gyms toward the parking lot. Ten minutes later, a mile west of town, on the hill where the Soo Line freight trains ran, a diesel locomotive hit its brakes too late to avoid destroying the compact car parked in the middle of the tracks.

My mother predicted the funeral would be crowded and that the cause of Mr. Hulbertson's suicide, and even the fact that it was a suicide, would probably go unmentioned—"To spare his memory." Then I shared with her some of my own memories, as well as my disgust with my hometown. I suspect that such conversations were common that day, but I don't know. Perhaps the silence held. In any case, like most of my old classmates, I skipped the service. My mother reported afterward that even more people attended than she'd anticipated and that the mood had been one of relief, of finally putting to rest a tortured soul. I set down my cup of coffee as she said this, rose from the kitchen table, left the house, and walked a few blocks to the town hall, a two-story white clapboard building with a bell tower, where I'd performed in *Tom Sawyer* as an eleven-year-old. Its doors were locked, both front and back, but I was able to climb over a gate and mount a staircase on the building's south side which led to a third door fitted with a window. I looked into the empty auditorium, at the century-old painted curtain in the front which depicted a summer river scene of paddlewheel steamboats sailing up a channel lined with leafy, overhanging trees. I thought back to the night I'd stood behind the curtain, huddling in the wings with Mr. Hulbertson as two of our class's strongest boys tugged hand over hand on a stout rope, revealing, in one continuous, long motion, an audience made up of everyone I knew. Their faces were smiling, their postures straight and patient, and on their laps and in their hands were white paper programs printed with all of our names.

Thrilling. Astonishing. It couldn't help but be.

Then my teacher touched one of my shoulders and I flinched.

"Tonight," he whispered to me and those around me as we peered out through our makeup at our town, "be proud of yourselves. That's all I ask. Is everyone ready?"

We touched our costumes, nodded.

"Terrific," he said. "Now go put on a show!"

# Chapter Six

My FATHER HAD A SPELL. HE QUIT 3M. HE DECIDED America's future lay out West, moved the family to Phoenix in a U-Haul, flew off to Tampa to watch his own dad die, lost weight, lost his marbles, opened the Yellow Pages, turned to a page headed "Churches," and called the Mormons. They came over right away. They came in the form of a pair of clean-cut missionaries with clip-on neckties and wrinkle-free white shirts. They asked us to kneel. They asked us to do a lot of things. There were also some things they asked us not to do. For me, the main one was to not touch myself. When we understood all the instructions, we were baptized. Then, a month later, my father bought some wine, which was one of the things he'd been asked not to do. His attitude was: "The Hell with it." Ours was: "Oh, God, what's going to happen now?" especially after my father lost his new job and called the Mayflower moving people. They parked a semitrailer in front of our house and loaded it full of our belongings, but my father couldn't tell them where to take them. He couldn't decide where we should move. He said he had a good feeling about Idaho, but he also retained a fondness for Minnesota. The Mayflower people grew impatient, pad-locked the trailer that held our stuff, detached the cab, and drove the cab away.

We lay on the floor of our empty house in sleeping bags while my father discussed his options. He only discussed them with himself. If someone else chimed in, he cut him off. The only times he left the house were to stand on the lawn and stare at the long trailer or walk around it in slow, deliberate circles, as though considering his options. My mother consoled herself with her Book of Mormon and quoted verses from it to my brother and me when we showed signs of panicking. Seeing her try to hold our family together, I realized I'd never appreciated her plight as the lonely bearer of aspirations for a more refined existence. When we'd first moved to Marine, she'd taught her-self French in her spare time, progressing from a series of cas-sette tapes to translations of Peanuts comic books to, after no more than a year or so, works by Voltaire, Balzac, and Camus. She repeated the feat with Italian later on, without neglecting her housework or her nursing career. And her interests also ran to subjects other than literature. Now and then I'd catch her in an armchair reading a popular history of philosophy by Will and Ariel Durant, and once, stacked high on the floor beside her bed, I found a complete edition, in many volumes, of *The Rise and Fall of the Roman Empire*, its pages abundantly marked by strips of paper covered in minutely lettered comments. Her feats of amateur scholarship were purely private, though, and they went undiscussed with the neighbors or the rest of us, though I sensed that she hoped they'd rub off on us someday, and espe-cially on me.

I was an eighth grader during our time in Phoenix, but

only technically, since I rarely attended school in those strange months. I did, though, participate in a spelling bee. I memorized a booklet of tricky words which competitive spellers often stumbled over, won the local round, won the district round, and advanced to the final round for all of Phoenix. A lot of my rivals on the stage were Asians. Asians scared me. I'd never spoken to one. Finally there were just two of us onstage, me and an Asian girl not half my height. My word was "villain," an easy one. I botched it. Nerves. The Asian girl didn't botch her word. She hugged my waist. Then she was mobbed by dozens of her kin.

I had only my father there. "You had to be perfect," he said. "You weren't quite perfect. Sometimes there's no in-between in life. I'm sorry."

When I did go to school, I rarely attended class, preferring to meet up in the parking lot with a quiet Hopi friend who led me all over Phoenix on his bike, showing me where his aunts and uncles lived, shouting threats when he passed a Navajo kid, and sometimes giving me one of the blue pills he kept in a Baggie in his shorts. The pills made me mournful. Mournful, but outgoing.

"What do you want to be someday?" I asked him.

"Hopi."

"You're Hopi now."

"And Hopi always."

"You want to know my goal?" I asked him.

He seemed indifferent.

"A newspaper columnist who gives opinions."

"Telling people what you think."

"Exactly."

"I hate to think. I like to see."

I might have avoided much sorrow down the line by adopting the outlook of my Hopi friend, but I didn't even get to say goodbye to him. When I got home that afternoon, the cab and the trailer were attached again and we were headed back to the Midwest. My mother had taken control. She'd called her father in Ohio, who'd called 3M in Minnesota and convinced them to give my father his old job back.

Weeks later, we bought our farm in Taylors Falls, a team of draft horses, some old machinery, a dozen chickens, a goat, and my father resumed his commute to the Twin Cities, stranding the rest of us in the nineteenth century and leaving my brother and me to the devices of one of Minnesota's lowest-ranked schools. Its dullness revived my interest in Mormonism.

The ward house was located in a St. Paul suburb. I dressed for services in burgundy loafers, a knit red tie, and a blue dress shirt whose stain-resistant finish reacted with sweat to create a spoiled-meat smell. By then my parents were drifting toward full apostasy (my little brother had dropped out entirely) and they only came to church when the bishop scheduled me to speak. In Phoenix, I'd become quite a Sunday speaker, and I got even better in St. Paul.

"To want what another has is to lose the bounty which Heavenly Father grants equally to all of us and cannot be added to, only subtracted from, never burnished but only soiled: the chance for our spirit to know Celestial glory and govern dominions of our own creation, much as Heavenly Father governs ours."

Establish a cadence, stretch it, vary it, return to it later in full force, and try not to think the words. That was the secret, I discovered. The words were interchangeable, anyway, particularly if they were fine or lofty words. "Holy," "sacred," "blessed," "delightsome," "pure." Their potency lay not in their meanings but in the patterns they cut into the air. When I was speaking in top form, these patterns seemed to precede the words, in fact, drawing them out of me like melodies writing their own lyrics.

"Brother Kirn, you had the Holy Spirit. I saw it. I heard it. And I thank you for it."

It wasn't good form to take such compliments personally; I always made sure to credit the Mormon deities. My real muses dwelt on a lower plane, however, in the seventh row of pews, stage right, where the church's trio of teenage beauties sat: Eliza, pristine and unattainable; Celia, restless and impressionable; and Kelly, whose nature blended the other girls', making her a favorite with the boys.

"You were perfect last week," she told me at a youth dance as "Nights in White Satin" heaved out of the speakers, simulating medievalism through overdubbing. "Want to smoke something illegal in my Dodge?"

"You liked my talk on backbiting that much?"

"It's your delivery, your energy. I loved how you barely stopped for breath except for that wonderful pause after 'incarnate.' Give me a minute's head start so no one catches us."

That's how my eloquence at church was graded: in parking-lot petting sessions, in wet French kisses. My school performance improved as a nice side effect and I was invited to join the declamation team by its chubby, mannish coach, Miss Normandy, who seemed to intuitively understand that speech and sex were linked for me. She let it be known that my teammates were all girls and that the regional tourney in Duluth involved an overnight stay in a motel. Of course I'd have to win district first, she said.

I did win, but not as handily as I'd hoped. My event, Small-Group Discussion, took place around an oval conference table that didn't suit the soaring speaking style I'd perfected at the altar. Here the trick was directness and flexibility as I jousted with my tablemates over the less-than-galvanizing issue of government funding for the arts. It alarmed me that two of my rivals wore three-piece suits and toted brown accordion file folders stuffed with documentation for their points. It occurred to me then for the first time that I was vying for the world's good things with a more cunning peer group than I'd realized, inside a broader, taller stadium.

"Subsidies, by removing risk," I said, "promote stagnation and suppress unorthodoxy." I'd emptied my clip in one big burst, an error. On my next turn to speak, I fired more slowly, with lower-caliber rounds. The judges scribbled on their clipboards, seeming to ratify my shift in tactics. It relaxed me to see this and boosted my confidence, which seemed to rattle the boys in suits. They clung to their note cards, spoke stiffly, forgot to gesture, and guaranteed me passage to the regionals.

I harmed myself the night before the match by staying up till dawn trying to walk off and bathe away the phosphorescent curlicues of dread loosed in my brain by a drugged cupcake I'd eaten with a teammate in her motel room. I hadn't fully recovered when I found myself battling a girl with close-set eyes and the excessively brushed straight hair of a virginal prodigy. Here was a force I'd never faced before: the supercharged purity of postponed puberty augmented by early viola training.

It rolled me over. "You're absolutely right, Kim. There's nothing I can add to what you've said."

Girl wonder seemed miffed at me. "You're conceding?"

"Yes."

I consoled myself for the loss with sacred oratory and carnal tussles in Kelly's Dodge, whose interior she'd regaled with cultic bric-a-brac: a pentagram medal on a silver chain, a black rabbit's foot dangling from the rearview mirror, Led Zeppelin decals in the corners of the windows. Such teeny-bopper occultism was rare with Mormon teens. The church gave the devil short shrift in its theology, diminishing his allure among young misfits.

"Why all the Lucifer?" I asked.

"Intelligence. He's the viceroy of intelligence."

I'd never heard this. "That's God, I thought."

"God created us to be obedient. Thought was the contribution of the Dark One."

"You're sure on that?"

"Read Genesis. Read *Steppenwolf.* You want to know what, Walter?"

"I do."

"I think you're one of His chosen. His elect. That's why you speak so well. He's in your brain."

I started avoiding Kelly after that. Her notion that I had a supernatural patron obliged me to dazzle her, I felt, to keep the flourishes and wonders coming. It was too much to live up to. And I was tiring of church, tiring of arranging rides to services and of having to cover my parents' absences with lies about health emergencies and such. I started spending more Sundays on the farm, directing my speeches on chastity and honor to our team of hulking Belgian mares. Sometimes, when they stamped their anvil feet, shivering the floorboards of their stalls, or loosed a long rolling shudder of dense muscle along their glossy flanks, I imagined they were responding to my eloquence. There was something at work in me, something strong and strange, and I wondered if Kelly's theory wasn't right. My father's behavior over the past year had shown me that people's wills can be invaded by inexplicable forces and agencies. I decided it might be time that I acknowledged them. Angels or devils? I didn't really care. I wanted them on my side, that's all I knew.

At the beginning of my tenth-grade year a large cardboard box marked FRAGILE arrived at school. It was brought to the classroom of Mr. Ka, our fussy Korean accounting instructor, and opened with razor blades by a pair of science teachers who behaved like archaeologists breaking the seal on an Egyptian tomb. After folding back the box's lid and peering inside for a few moments as though considering how best to proceed, they gingerly removed its contents: a slightly smaller box, this one made of Styrofoam. Mr. Ka's tense face drew tighter still as the razor blades were deployed again, but when the precious cargo was finally liberated, swept clean of foam crumbs and placed upon his desk, he beamed like a kid who'd asked Santa for a sled and been given a working flying saucer.

The thing was a computer—the first one designed for use by average people, according to Mr. Ka. He said that few schools of our size, or any size, were fortunate enough to own one yet, meaning that we, his students, would get a "major head start on the future" when we became familiar with the device. And we shouldn't be fooled by its modest size, he said. Inside this machine lay the power of a thousand, maybe ten thousand pocket calculators. Inside this machine was the potential to generate telephone directories for America's ten most populous cities. Inside this machine were lucrative careers for everybody in this room.

"So tomorrow," he said, "we get started on tomorrow."

It was a slow start; so slow it wasn't a start. Our first problem—and our last one, it turned out; indeed, our *only* one—was philosophical. How could we know if the thing was working properly before we knew how it worked or how to work it? We read our computer books, hunting for the answers, searching for clues as to what the answers might look like, hunting for terms and phrases and sentences comprehensible to people who didn't already know the answers. We read the books individually and silently, meaning that there was no way to determine who among us was just pretending to read them in the hope that others would actually read them and explain their findings to the rest of us. I was one of the real readers at first, but when I realized I wasn't making headway, I became one of the simulated readers. By scratching my chin and glancing off into space and generally appearing vexed and baffled, I labored to make my act convincing, which I felt was my duty to anyone still persevering toward our goal. My feigned struggles might give them heart, or shame them out of quitting. Either way, the chances might increase that someday someone in Mr. Ka's computer class would bring the inert beige box to life.

But there was no evidence that anyone read the books.

While we waited to learn to program by inspiration, we sought a breakthrough using trial and error. The effort failed because we lacked a usable definition of error. That's when we stopped touching the device and chose to regard it as an icon or a totem. Our classes turned into speculative chats about the wonders the object might perform if instead of addressing it in COBOL or FORTRAN, we could interact with it in English. To heighten the atmosphere of possibility, we kept the thing plugged in. This warmed its obscurely coiled and bundled insides, releasing unappetizing chemical vapors.

"Say we could feed it every single play in Osceola's offensive playbook. Maybe it would think up perfect defensive plays. And say it was hooked to earphones in our helmets and told us exactly how to run them. We might take state next year."

Mr. Ka looked from Nils, the speaker, our starting center linebacker, to me, an occasional blocker during punt returns. "Assuming the Apple could do that, how would *you* feel?"

"Happy. Great. Why not?"

"You wouldn't feel . . . *humbled*?"

"I would," said Pat, another starting player. He was stretched out at his desk beside the mechanism, moving one hand in circles above its head as though polishing its invisible halo. "I'd feel like, hey, I'm not needed, why play football? Why get your bell rung and bruise your shins instead of just goofing off with Pac-Man and drinking an ice-cold Schlitz?"

"Hey, I know," a guy said. "Picture this, okay?" He stood and approached the Apple with widespread arms, softly fluttering his hands, like wings. It was a courtship dance, it seemed. "We win its trust. We come in peace, we tell it. We want it to help us read coma victims' minds, say, or write another Shakespeare play. Then, very slowly, careful not to scare it, we reach out for its little plastic throat"—he curved his hands into a choking position—"and throttle it till it starts to spark and shit.

Smoke rolls out of it, bells ring, sirens wail. The cockpits of jet planes go haywire, they explode, missile silos open by themselves, and a dozen Chinese robots go berserk and kill all the pandas at the zoo."

"My hour hand just hit ten," said Mr. Ka. "Tomorrow, gentlemen. Excellent. Most excellent. We didn't waste our time today."

A month or two into the class I grew dissatisfied. Yes, they were pleasant, our hours of dreamy bullshit, and yes, the Apple was quite a talisman, but did our mutual agreement to give up trying to operate the thing mean, perhaps, that the world had changed around us while we, for the first time in our young lives, had rejected change? It hadn't been this way during the Apollo years. We'd built model rockets then, we'd studied weightlessness. Shouldn't we be taking that approach? Perhaps, but we were uninspired. Computers, larger models than the Apple, existed already and other people ran them, a situation we found acceptable because it allowed us the freedom to live in ignorance while receiving the benefits of modernization. We were only sixteen but somehow we'd grown old.

"This is Jason, class," said Mr. Ka late in the semester. The boy was a tadpole-shaped twelve-year-old, all head. "Jason will help us relate to the computer."

"It's pretty outrageous, this machine," said Jason. "Move your chairs in. Form a circle, guys."

The exhibition unveiled no technical mysteries, but it did help me understand the term "conservative" as I'd once heard it used by a friend's father while he was watching the TV news. A conservative was a person who stopped adjusting once adjustment brought him no vital benefits. The commandment to us from kindergarten on had been to grow, to expand ourselves, to stretch, but there was another option, too, I saw. One could let others cope with novelty and concentrate on the familiar.

Jason continued trying to excite us. He divided a string of numbers that ran all the way to the right side of a notebook page by another monstrous sum which started with ten or twelve zeros behind a decimal point behind a minus sign. The printer was already printing out the answer while most of us were still mocking the equation, and it was at this instant that I became something I couldn't name till later: a student of the liberal arts, devoted to concepts and ideas which didn't depend on disembodied logic, on greater-than signs and parentheses and ampersands. This decision guided my studies from then on. The hard sciences were just too hard for me.

"Hey Jason," said one of my buddies to the whiz kid over hamburger salad at lunch one day. "Ever have a girlfriend?"

"What do you think?"

"You're *twelve*. Get with it."

"Eleven and a half."

"Ever *want* a girlfriend?"

"What do you think?"

"Processing. Thinking. Tabulating. Printing." This was me, satirizing Jason's thinking in a cartoonish, transistorized monotone. "Conclusion: Negative. Categorically." Then I switched over to my natural voice. "Jason, your new name is Neuter Nine." Then back to a female version of the main voice. "Testicular excision now commencing. Working. Working. Surgery complete."

Jason went on eating his hot lunch. He hadn't flinched. I hadn't made him cry. Until then, I'd merely considered him ridiculous. Now I feared him. I rose and took my tray to a table across the room. I had a book with me. I pretended to read it. The others could have their weird symbols. I'd take words.

For me, the remainder of high school was a drinking party held in a cabin beside a lake, followed by three or four months of casual reading in world almanacs. I had some idea that a head all full of facts might smooth my transition into college now that my SAT results were in and the brochures were pouring into my mailbox. When Macalester said I could skip my senior year, I started saying goodbye to people. The rubber-gloved lunch ladies. Mr. Ka. The janitors. It was all over school that I wasn't coming back.

My last, most uncomfortable goodbye was to Mr. C., the English teacher whose wife's first pregnancy had forced him to quit the grad-school program that he hoped would turn him into a novelist. I'd started ducking him way back in the winter, declining an invitation to an Eagles show and not responding either way to his assertion that it would be a gas to eat a dozen peyote buttons and go to a late show of *Saturday Night Fever*. When he tried to reestablish contact by biking over to our farm one weekend and coaxing me into getting high while I brushed and groomed the horses, I told him I'd only take one hit because I was feeling guilty as a Mormon.

Now it was time to pay him a final call. I drove to his modular house one Sunday evening, walked up the gravel path past his kids' yard toys—plastic tricycles, deflated basketballs—and knocked on his hollow-feeling vinyl door. His wife let me in. Around her and behind her were three or four fussy infants and toddlers. In the back of the room was her husband in his recliner wearing sunglasses, reading a book of poetry.

"Walt, the new Dire Straits came. Come on in. You'll want to hear two of the tracks on headphones first."

"I can't really stay."

"Miller High Life, can or bottle?"

"Can," I said. A beer can is opaque. You don't have to drink it to the bottom.

"I heard you just *crushed* those college boards."

"I guess I have a knack for multiple choice."

He held out the headphones with their ear cups spread. I smelled wet diapers and wanted to get away.

"Macalester took you. I heard that, too," he said.

"I'm thinking I might only spend a year there. I'd like to go somewhere out East if I can swing it." Then I decided to ask the question that was my real reason for dropping over. Mr. C. was the only person I knew who might be able to answer it.

"Is Harvard the top or is all of that just talk?"

"Yes, it's the top, but the talk is why it is. That's how engineered hysteria operates. That's why the Ivy League doesn't fear encroachment by the Soybean Alliance or Coal Confederation. It trains its students to spread its propaganda, which attracts even brighter students who go on spreading it."

"What about Williams College? They sent a pamphlet."

"I see you at Reed College in Portland, Oregon."

"Why?"

"It's where I went. A little intense but not obnoxious. Though I guess you could also try Princeton, where your dad went."

"No one knows that. How do you?"

"I asked him in a parent-teacher conference. It surprised me. I thought he was lying. I wouldn't have guessed."

"Fitzgerald studied at Princeton. I've read Fitzgerald."

"Except that he barely studied. And didn't graduate. Eugene O'Neill, the same. They kicked him out. I'd be suspicious of a place like that. If you want to crawl drunk and naked through the snow after being raped by your best friend, there's always Yale, of course."

I looked at my wrist as though I wore a watch but had forgotten to put it on that day. Our talk had grown dispiriting.

"Another Miller?" said Mr. C. "I dug up a British Hendrix bootleg that'll melt your temples through those headphones."

I rose from the couch without signaling or asking. Mr. C. looked resigned. He stood up, too. We'd had a few good times together, but I was absorbed in my plans now, and he knew it. He knew he'd been just a stop along the way.

"Well, wherever you go," he said, "skip the drinking games, don't buy acid or uppers on the street, and always—I want you to promise—wear a rubber. Even if her daddy's very rich."

"I'll keep that in mind," I said. "Funny."

"Now get out of here."

And that's exactly what I did.

The year before I left for Princeton, during my last semester at Macalester, something happened to remind me that I'd chosen correctly in leaving the Midwest. My high school invited me back for senior prom as a sort of returning celebrity and I was given a choice of two exchange students as dates for the upcoming dance. One, a French girl, Genevieve, was conventionally pretty, with the sort of brown skin that looks fine with a few moles on it and isn't terribly marred by a dark hair or two. The second girl, Lena, my favorite, was a lithe, unblemished stunner whose skin seemed dusted in powdered gold. I don't remember her country of origin. It was one of those small, frigid nations that at the time was partly subjugated by the Russians but would eventually break free and dominate the worldwide modeling scene.

The reason I had the choice of the two girls was that they intimidated my male classmates, who sensed—correctly, I think—that the exchange students abhorred our monotonous rural culture and were counting the hours until they could jet home to the bastions of strong dark coffee and avant-garde theater where they'd been raised and educated. The girls, it seemed clear to us, had lost some lottery that had assigned their more fortunate peers to such hot spots as Florida and San Francisco. The idea was that we were to play ambassadors to this pair of lovely travelers, convincing them of the United States' benevolent, easygoing character, but instead our high school found their presence embarrassing, perhaps because they spoke better English than most of us and seemed caught up in issues of global concern about which we had scant knowledge and few opinions.

I was considered the exception. I liked the girls and was thought by my shy friends to have something in common with them because I was already enrolled in college and had learned there to talk politics, which allowed me to voice polite agreement with their uncharitable assessments of "America's cultural imperialism." The only problem, as the prom approached, was

that I couldn't imagine choosing Lena—my clear favorite between the girls—without offending Genevieve. When I let Lena
in on my dilemma, she failed to see the trouble: we should attend as a group, she said, a trio. My face remained still as we
talked this notion over, but behind my brow strange thoughts
unfolded, dim scenarios of new behaviors, of unfamiliar sensa-
tions, exotic postures. I began to sense that my small-town high-
school prom—my symbolic farewell to the Midwest—would
also be my introduction to a welcome new life of cosmopolitan
decadence.

Accompanied by my two dates, the drive from the dance in
the school gymnasium to the after party at a lake took about
three hours—hours I can't account for except as a drastic recon-
figuration of my accumulated heartland notions about "going all
the way." I recall specifically a big, sweet slug of syrupy fruit
wine that passed from mouth to mouth and then was allowed to
stream down a bare chin onto a pair of dark breasts with perfect
moles, which snagged the liquid in glinting droplets that I was
invited to lightly tongue away while another tongue, and then
another, shaped themselves into slim, wet, fleshy cones and
drove themselves deep, deep into my ear canals. Skirts came up,
pants slipped off, and legs made V's that turned into X's and
shifted on complex axes that allowed for wonders of sidelong
friction that brought forth fetching squeaks and grunty purrs
that primordially bridged all language gaps. Some new bond was
being stirred in that car, some fresh form of international understanding that the Rotary Club, or whichever organizations
sponsored the exchange program, might not have planned on
but shouldn't have been displeased by, so intimately did it shrink
our globe. I'd grown up a good son of rural Republican Min-

nesota, but now I was a citizen of the world. When we finally reached the party we smelled like sin, and not American sin but a deep-brewed funk of Romanized corruption that caused me to compulsively sniff my hands whenever I lifted my cup to sip my beer.

My buddies swarmed in to share their prom-night war stories, and my girls slipped away past the bonfire into the trees, leaving me alone to contemplate—with the distaste and contempt that I assumed they suffered from every moment of their visits here—just how stupid Minnesota was. How stupid we all were, here in crass America. Everywhere I looked I saw the evidence. The barbarous chest-pounding of our square-jawed prom king as he bellowed "Seniors rule!" across the lake. The way the homely girl we'd nicknamed "Critter," and who pathetically answered to the name, sat alone and shoeless on a log, dipping her toes in the froggy, fetid water. And the music! The music was the worst. Ted Nugent blaring at teeth-rattling volume from the tape deck of someone's flame-streaked red Camaro. How had I ever borne this gruesome exile?

I went off to look for my tutors in exoticism. I stepped on Styrofoam beer cups that loudly crunched and would never, I knew from science class, decompose, but would junk up our sacred earth for a thousand years. A drunk girl whose breasts I'd crudely mashed and squeezed once during a nighttime bus trip from a speech event sloppily grabbed my crotch and slurped my cheeks with a tongue that smelled like menthol cigarettes. As I twisted away from her, she said, "Not good enough for you, am I, college boy?" I didn't correct her. It wasn't nice, I knew, but sometimes the truth is the truth and can't be helped.

# Seven

My first semester at Princeton I had four roommates who resembled no one I'd ever known: Peter, a foppish piano prodigy with a mature, fine-bristled mustache, who dreamed of writing Broadway musical comedies and spent his leisure time in a robe and slippers, smoking Benson and Hedges Menthol 100s and hunching, vulturelike, over his black Steinway, plinking out show tunes about doe-eyed ingenues who'd been seduced and ruined by caddish tycoons. Jennifer, the composer's plump heiress girlfriend, whose father owned a night club and often sent a limousine on weekends so that his daughter could party with celebrities, who—as I learned from a framed snapshot which sat on a dresser in her and Peter's bedroom—included the two best-known members of the Bee Gees. Tim, the son of a New York journalist, who kept his cheeks fresh with Oil of Olay and treated the composer and the heiress as surrogate parents, addressing them in baby talk and asking them to tuck him in at night, which they did, complete with fairy tales. And Joshua, an earnest Long Island Quaker kid with a close-trimmed, pious-seeming red beard, who played guitar and protested apartheid, which I pretended to be concerned about, too, although I wasn't certain what it was. The SATs hadn't required such trivial knowledge.

One night a report came over the radio that John Lennon, Joshua's hero, had been assassinated. We were lying on our bunks in the small bedroom that we shared at the far end of the suite, around the corner from a dank bathroom which smelled of wet feet and backed-up drains. My other three roommates slept closer to the common room, a bright south-facing sitting area neutrally furnished with nicked-up chairs and tables and a tough old institutional sofa whose denim-covered cushions hid a thick layer of pennies, ash, and paper clips. The suite was located in Wilson College, the ugliest cluster of buildings on the campus and the home to an inordinate number of glum-looking black and Jewish kids. That I, an unconnected transfer student, had ended up in Wilson was not surprising, but my Manhattan roommates seemed offended at having been assigned such modest quarters.

"Lennon. Dead," said the radio. "Imagine."

The first report, and the many that followed it, plunged Joshua into fits of heaving grief. "They finally did it," he moaned. "They finally got him." Lennon's untimely demise meant little to me thanks to my heavy-metal upbringing (I hadn't even known, before that night, that he'd gone on writing and recording after he left the Beatles), but I could tell from Joshua's stricken eyes that something momentous had occurred, a catastrophe which, in the words of one announcer, would "devastate an entire generation," and I wanted in on the cosmopolitan trauma. I saw the event as a chance to put behind me my provincial, mass-market sensibilities and join the ranks of the discerning elect.

"Let's sing something. 'Working Class Hero,'" I said to Joshua, squeezing a few thin tears through my dry ducts. I hadn't heard of the song before that night but the radio people were making fancy claims for it, calling it one of Lennon's most "personal statements" and an "enduring critique of fame itself."

"I'd rather play another one. It's for the young man, the poor killer," said Quaker Joshua. He settled his shaky fingers on the guitar strings, strummed a chord, fell silent, sighed, then rallied.

"*All the lonely people,*" he began.

The choice was a magical piece of luck for me. Afterward, spent, having sung with my whole rib cage and fully emoted on every memorized word, I felt the urge to cry for real—from gratitude. Thanks to my gloomy second-grade music teacher, I'd managed to respond convincingly, in the company of a well-credentialed witness, to a historic cultural tragedy that would be revisited for decades. My genuine tears flowed along with my false tears, and as they did the distinction between them blurred. I wasn't ashamed of this. My fraudulence, I was coming to understand, was in a way the truest thing about me. It represented ambition, longing, need. It sprung from the deepest chambers of my soul.

"Somehow it's going to turn out okay," said Joshua. "Somehow we're going to come through this."

"Let's hope," I said.

———

I needed a good cry that night for other reasons. I'd needed one for weeks.

It had all started one Sunday afternoon when Jennifer, the heiress, returned from a weekend city trip accompanied by a uniformed driver who was lugging a case of champagne her father had given her. I watched from my bedroom doorway, thinking: I live with people who have servants. When Jennifer saw me loitering, unoccupied, she invited me into the common room where we popped the cork on a green bottle and drank the bubbly without glasses, licking the foam when it ran down the neck. This struck me as the height of decadence and reason enough for betraying my hometown buddies, with whom I'd promised to keep in touch but hadn't. I'd heard from my mother that a couple of them were in the army now, stationed in Korea and Germany, and that one had hitchhiked to Alaska to labor in a salmon cannery. Another guy from Taylors Falls, a famously volatile delinquent who used to call in bomb threats to the school, had married and fathered a child by a farm girl who suffered from a form of dwarfism. Her doctors had warned them that giving birth might kill her but my friend had received a message from God, reportedly, assuring him that she'd survive. The delivery proved complicated and costly, and to cover the bills my friend had taken a job disposing of dangerous industrial wastes. The work had required him to wear a spacesuit, but the outfit hadn't functioned well, apparently, and now he was ailing, unemployed, and, rumor had it, headed for divorce.

"What are you?" Jennifer asked me as we drank. "This is an arts room. What's your bag? Your talent?"

"I've written a bit of experimental poetry."

"To me you look more like a . . . Let me think. A playwright."

I grinned from cheek to blushing cheek, flattered that I looked like anything to someone who consorted with the Bee Gees.

"I think it's the way your hair sticks up," said Jennifer. "Playwrights are generally terribly unkempt. It's all they can do to shave and not catch crabs."

"Really? I've never heard that," I said. "Why?"

"Why are most virtuoso violinists perverted sex fiends? Because they are," she said. "Why are all newspaper people disgusting drunks?"

"You've seen a lot," I said.

"I've seen it all. I've seen it from the front and from the back."

"What are the Bee Gees like?"

"Normal. Nice. You'd like them."

Was this a promise? I could only hope. It didn't seem like an outlandish hope, though. The friends of one's friends very often became one's own friends—time and proximity were all it took. I slugged back more wine to cool my burning brain. A diploma, I was starting to see, was the least of what Princeton had to offer; the major payoff was front-row seats. To everything. But what would they cost? I suspected they might be free. Something told me that people such as Jennifer didn't obtain admission to things with tickets; they were ushered in through secret entrances, through fire exits and stage doors, and their guests were permitted to sweep on in behind them.

To consolidate what I believed to be my progress toward someday unwinding backstage with global pop stars, I asked

Jennifer about her family history, guessing that ownership of a top hotel wasn't an overnight achievement. I was rewarded with a saga of American commercial striving which commenced at the end of the last century and took in the construction of famous bridges, the invention of basic industrial materials, the compounding of fortunes through advantageous marriages, and the advent of the modern theme park. Jennifer introduced the epic's cast with a certain formality, by their full names, including their middle and maiden names, but after a while she relaxed and the demigods became "Harold," "Old Bill," "Great-Gran." Her story had a strange effect on me. It made me feel trusted, included, but also belittled, particularly when Jennifer called her family "my people" or "the clan." I had no clan, of course, and I knew there was little chance I ever would, since such lineages took ages to mature, as did the investments they were founded on. Yes, I could start on the project in a few years, and with luck it might still be advancing when I died, but I'd never know its ultimate fate. Jennifer obviously realized this, because she asked not one question about my background after she finished mythologizing hers.

When we'd drained the champagne, she said, "You owe me twenty."

I stared at her, uncomprehending. "For what?" I said.

"That was an excellent label. You owe me twenty. Though actually who you owe it to is Daddy."

I didn't have the money, and I said so. My parents sent checks now and then, but not for much; they lacked any sense of the cost of living at Princeton. My phone bills alone consumed most of their remittances, freezing me out of any real social life and limiting my wardrobe to a pair of wrinkled Levi's corduroys, a blue pocket T-shirt with a torn armpit, a white Oxford dress shirt I never wore, and one red, lumberjacky flannel number, which filled me with shame about my regional origins. My Adidas sneakers were fashionable enough, but they weren't the scuffed-up leather Top-Siders favored by the breezy gentry.

"Welsher," said Jennifer, putting me in my place. In Minnesota, I hadn't had a place, but here I did: several levels down from heiresses who charged their roommates to drink free wine. It seemed unfair that I had come so far in life only to find new ways to fall short.

"I'll pay you next week," I said.

"We'll just forget it."

"I don't *want* to forget it."

"Tough," said Jennifer. Then she gave me the bottle to throw away.

Week by week, the humiliations mounted. While reading Tim his bedtime story one night, Jennifer was forced to take a phone call and she asked me to fill in. The book was *The Little Prince*, in French, and Tim wound up having to read it to himself, throwing his baby voice through a stuffed koala worn down practically furless from years of hugging. Soon afterward, a friend of Peter's from Boston invited me to join him for a squash game. No racket, though. And no idea what one might look like.

Then came the business of the furniture.

Returning from classes one afternoon, past the fat gray squirrels all nervous with their nuts, the squads of leggy female runners with sweaty ponytails flopping against their necks, the imperturbable immigrant science profs attentive only to their inner reveries, the rumbling riding mowers of the grounds crew vacuuming up dry leaves through their attachments, I was feeling vaguely content about the fact that I'd survived another day without exposing my naked ignorance when I noticed a Bloomingdale's delivery van parked on the sidewalk outside my dormitory. Its broad rear doors were open wide and its loading ramp was down, a pair of dollies with heavy canvas straps lying beside it on the chilly ground among a litter of empty cardboard cartons.

Inside, in the common room, two burly workers were taking orders from Peter, who was in his robe on the piano bench, an ashtray balanced on one of his crossed knees. The workers had brought in new armchairs, plant stands, lamps, a coffee table, a large TV set, and a voluptuous chintz sofa, setting them all on a Persian rug so vast that its edges curled up against the walls, blocking the electrical outlets. There were also white lace curtains on the windows and the floral smell of scented candles. The old institutional decor had vanished, replaced with what looked like a set from an old movie about the lives of refined young socialites.

My instinct when I came upon this scene was to pass by in silence, brow scrunched and eyes averted, and hide out in my hovel of a bedroom, whose only improvement was a plastic bookcase fashioned from milk crates I'd found behind a dining hall. I didn't know exactly what was happening, only that it had happened without me, and not by accident, I presumed. I poked my head out the door at dinnertime but the sight of my roommates enjoying their plush new setup, champagne flutes raised, their faces bright and rosy, drove me back into protective seclusion. To block out the wickedness of their laughing voices I put an album on Joshua's stereo—an early Bob Dylan record, full of lonesome ballads and drawling reproaches to the power structure.

"We figured out everyone's part in this whole thing," Peter informed me the next morning as I tried to slip past him and out the door. He was watching the *Today* show with Tim and Jennifer, all of them snugly embedded in the new sofa and showing no sign they intended to go to classes or do anything but drink tea all day and snicker. "Your share is six hundred and seventy," he said.

"My share of what?"

"Our new living room," said Tim.

"But I didn't order any of this stuff."

"Well, you'll benefit from it, won't you?" Jennifer said.

This was my first brush with a line of reasoning that would echo through my years at Princeton: even unbidden privileges must be paid for. Tuition, the university liked to tell us, covered only a fraction of the cost of students' educations. What's more, the benefits of a Princeton degree were so far-reaching and long-lasting, supposedly, that for the duration of our lives we would be expected to give money to various university funds and causes, all of which were portrayed as critical to carrying out what was called the place's "mission." I'd assumed that a deal was a deal when Princeton admitted me, but I was mistaken, it turned out. The price of getting in—to the university itself, and to the presumed wonderland it led to—would be an endless dunning for nebulous services that weren't included in the prospectus.

My roommates kept pestering me but I stood firm. I told them I couldn't pay and wouldn't pay. I told them there was a principle at stake, though I wasn't quite certain which one. It felt like more than one. After a while they stopped approaching me and convened a meeting in the common room—to discuss my "recalcitrance," they said. I sat out the proceedings in my bedroom as Joshua strummed a brooding Neil Young song about Cortés, the brutal Spanish explorer, and all the natives he'd smoothly decimated. Joshua had paid his bill without a fuss, it seemed, which struck me as an egregious violation of his solemn Quaker duty to resist unjust authority. I didn't press this point, however. The atmosphere in the suite was tense enough by then, and I needed a friend and ally, however meek. Or maybe he wasn't meek at all, maybe he'd mastered the art of wise acceptance, bending like the willow, Quaker style, and rendering unto Caesar, etcetera. We certainly seemed to be surrounded by Romans.

Tim delivered the verdict after the meeting. He addressed me in his unfamiliar adult voice, which sounded as phony as his baby voice, all husky and burred and ripped off from the movies. I was banned, he declared, from touching any item that I had not bought stock in. This included the Persian rug. Did I understand? I said I did. The necessity of avoiding the vast silk rug would place the entire common room off-limits to me, confining me to my sleeping quarters, the bathroom, and the hallway that ran to the front door.

The suite was now a concentrated version of what the whole campus would come to represent for me: a private association of the powerful which I'd been invited to visit on a day pass that, I sensed, might be revoked at any time as arbitrarily as it had been issued. I lay on my bunk that night and raged inside, sinking at last into a seething sleep that was the opposite of rest.

Instead of dreams I had metaphysical wrestling matches with disembodied oppressors. I woke up with blood on my front teeth, having bitten or chewed a hole in my tongue tip. The next few nights were just as black and taxing. By the weekend I'd developed a rolling twitch, a sort of chronic electrical disturbance, deep in the calf muscles of both my legs. When I tried to massage away the spasms, they spread to my thighs, then up into my hips. I started taking aspirin with every meal, switching to Tylenol when aspirin hurt my stomach. I borrowed a book on Buddhism from the library, learned the rudiments of meditation, and even devised a mantra for myself, "Ormalatala," a string of nonsense syllables that sounded as if they ought to soothe me but made me feel silly, desperate, and unhinged.

The one thing I didn't try was disobedience. I reacted to the new charter by strictly heeding it, thinking this might draw attention to its absurdity. I limited my movements to the traffic lanes, looking away when the TV was on and laying not a toe upon the rug. My wardens ignored me, unembarrassed, strangers both to pity and to shame. Two weeks after sending me into outer darkness, they started throwing big parties in the common room, setting out trays of vegetables and cheeses and mixing cocktails from a well-stocked bar whose bottles and glasses had arrived by limousine. The guests were giddy campus drama types, mostly from New York City or its best suburbs, who seemed to have known one another, in many cases long before they entered Princeton, through a network of New England summer arts camps directed by luminaries I'd seen in magazines and couldn't imagine stooping to teach teenagers. The party guests looked at me with shining eyes and curious faces as I trod silently past them to the bathroom or darted, head down and sheepish, into my bedroom. What did they think was my problem, or did they know?

One night a dark-haired junior named Nina, an established director at Princeton's Theatre Intime, shadowed me to my bedroom. She plunked down a whiskey sour on my desk next to the Hermes manual typewriter which held a page from a play I'd started writing about the president and his top national security aide. Making up lines for imaginary people eased the spasms in my legs, I'd found. As long as I was them, I wasn't me, and as long as I wasn't me, I didn't twitch.

"You're fond of stichomythia," said Nina, straightening and reading the curled page. "You're a Beckett fan, obviously. Or is it Pinter?"

I let these baffling allusions ride.

"What's it about?"

"Armageddon."

"In what respect?"

"Pretty much all of them," I said.

Nina sat down with her drink on Joshua's mattress in a manner that showcased her black stockings and the red straps that hooked them to her garter belt. Her skirt was made of wet-looking black vinyl, a fabric I'd only seen once, on a TV show, worn by a foxy LA vice cop working undercover as a prostitute.

"I know why you're not at the party. Infantile. If it makes you feel any better, they're clowns. They're hacks. Their idea of a show is girls in tights, kicking their pretty ankles above their heads."

I toasted this insult with my plastic cup. Nina's black turtle-neck tightened across her chest as she returned the gesture. I could tell she'd grown up in New York like all the rest of them, and I thought I could even guess which neighborhood: the Upper West Side. One of her parents was probably a professor, of history or philosophy, most likely. Childhood trips to Florence and Madrid, a fondness for Jamaican reggae, and a sibling who was in trouble with the law thanks to a weakness for heroin or gambling. Just a few months after leaving my small town, I was becoming an expert social bird-watcher. And there weren't all that many species, I'd discovered—not, at least, among the Princeton art crowd. There were the somber iconoclasts like Nina, children of darkest intellectual Europe, and the exuberant show-offs like my roommates, who reveled in spectacle and song. My natural loyalties were with the first group, but not because I understood their premises. I liked them because they disliked the others, as I did.

By the time Nina left to fetch us two fresh drinks, I sensed that she found my outcast status intriguing and fancied herself a sort of exile, too, as wasn't uncommon, I'd find out, with kids who'd been raised at the center of everything. An hour later I was lying on top of her in a cold off-campus communal house which reeked of hashish, crème de menthe, and brown bananas. On the cracked stucco walls were unframed student paintings whose abstract muddiness irked me for some reason. My lovemaking was brisk, ungenerous. This suited Nina just fine. "You're good," she said. "You know how to take, to be selfish. I guessed right."

"How?" I said.

"The beautiful wild fury behind your eyes."

That Nina had seen my anger surprised me. Ever since being booted from the common room, I'd labored to hide my wrath under a smirk so as not to gratify my enemies. With

Nina's wet breath roaring warmly in my ear canals, I decided to change this policy. Raw disgruntlement was rare at Princeton, and some people found it beguiling, it seemed. "Play your best card," my father had always said. Mine would be an ace of spades. A black ace.

Dating Nina raised my profile in serious campus drama circles and brought support for the staging of my play: *Late Modern, an Apocalyptic Comedy*. My roommates were unmoved by my step up and didn't admit me to their get-togethers—their "salons," as they'd begun to call them. Nina was no longer welcome at them, either. The wonder was that she ever had been. Her spare, dimly lit productions of Beckett's *Endgame* and Ionesco's *Rhinoceros* were, according to Peter, "utter masturbatory anarchy." I didn't entirely disagree with him. Nina's theatrical hero, I'd discovered, was a mad Frenchman, Antonin Artaud, whose writings suggested that the ideal play ought to resemble a sort of torchlit orgy climaxing in a crackdown by the police.

My piece was staged in an airless black-box theater tucked beneath a campus rec room stuffed with clacking foosball tables and beeping Space Invaders consoles. The director was Adam, whom I'd met through Nina, who'd begun taking credit for my ascent while privately telling me, "You'll choke. You'll blow this." She had good reason to be concerned. On rehearsal nights, before the cast arrived, Adam and I would push thin coffee straws through the drilled-out rubber stopper of an ampoule of pure liquid cocaine which he'd pilfered from a New York hospital where he'd worked as an orderly that summer. The drugs, we thought, sharpened our vision of the production, but they also prevented us from clearly conveying it to our two main actors, who rolled their eyes at our psychedelic suggestions to "lead with your auras," "float above the lines," "gesture negatively through stillness," and "turn every pause into a small inferno."

One night my lead, my President, a sorrowful tall Southerner named Reynolds who seemed to be at Princeton on the strength of having carried the antique gene for tubercular romantic wispiness into modern times, mounted a polite aesthetic mutiny.

"The script has weaknesses. It's thin. A tissue. It's part an homage to Kubrick's *Dr. Strangelove*—"

"A movie," I said, "which of course I've never seen."

"You must have. Believe me. You've just forgotten. My obsession with purity, my hypochondria, that's one hundred percent out of the film."

"Maybe some of it, twenty minutes, on TV once."

"And part a stereotypical revue sketch on erotically blocked religious maniacs."

"I was a Mormon, Reynolds. These aren't stereotypes. I had a bishop in my early teens whose remedy for my dirty thoughts—no lie—was buying a *Playboy*, tearing out the centerfold, and drawing wounds on it, gaping bloody wounds, with a red Magic Marker."

"I'm sorry you went through that. My largest concern is not the content, though. It's the shape of the play. The narrative skeleton."

I nodded to show respect for his concern, then blew out a roiling plume of cigarette smoke into the beam of a high-intensity can light.

"You're saying it's cloud-shaped. A swirl. A nebula."

"I'm saying nothing. I'm letting physics speak for me."

"So what's my goal in this thing? My inner arc?"

"To launch a nuclear missile, call God to earth, and usher in the age of peace and love. It might be a dream, though. A hallucination. Happening not in the White House to the president but to a patient in an asylum."

"I can't even tell you how often that's been done. It's like when the Martians invade and people panic, except it turns out they've come to teach, to heal."

"Maybe. But not to my knowledge," I said.

"Then get more knowledge. Please."

"Stand on your tape mark and wait till Adam gets back. Practice your speech about when you were a kid and blew up a firecracker in your hand that left a round scar like the sky wheel in Ezekiel."

I'd put down the revolt, but I was rattled. I stopped attending rehearsals. When I learned that my roommates had all bought tickets to the opening performance, I begged Adam to call off the production, but his drug-stoked momentum was unstoppable. "We're here to disturb, not impress or please," he said. "And the play's not just yours now. It's all of ours. It's its. It belongs to itself. It's a creature with a will. You need to drop the leash and let it run."

"The coke's all gone, isn't it? Let me see the ampoule."

Adam tapped a finger on his forehead. "Metabolized, not gone."

My adversaries took seats in the third row, their playbills neatly settled on their laps, their postures preposterously magisterial, as though they were overseeing a war-crimes trial. I lurked in the back against an exit door. The shudders rippled down my thighs and calves as though my legs were being unzipped. The disasters materialized early. The President skipped an entire page of dialogue only a minute or two into the show, while the National Security Adviser absently twisted a pinkie in his left ear during a speech that was intended by the author as a symphonic lamentation over our hunger for belief, for faith, and the dangers posed by the fact that we never feel full. There were technical issues, too. The lighting guy, who'd eaten a hash brownie which he'd sworn would wear off before the show, toggled at random between clashing colors, turning the stage into a cruise-ship disco, and during the silences between big lines misfired foosballs from the upstairs lounge bounced on the ceiling, as sharp as hammer strikes, then rolled along endlessly above our heads in grainy, resonant acoustic detail.

The audience didn't seem to mind, though. There was even a fair amount of laughter. It came in different spots than I'd anticipated, but this made it no less heartening to me. Indeed, it seemed to bear out Adam's theory about the way that plays escape their masters.

People patted my shoulder as they left. I even got several kisses on both cheeks from stylish upperclassmen. My roommates' reactions were stingy and oblique but nothing like the sharp lashes I'd expected. Jennifer winked in the way that people do when they want you to lie in bed all night wondering exactly what they meant. Peter said, "Not at all a total debacle." Tim turned and faced me as though he planned to speak but instead he tapped me on the breastbone with a tightly rolled-up playbill, either granting me a kind of knighthood or threatening me with Mafia violence—I couldn't tell. Which I knew was what he wanted.

Feeling content, then jaunty, then philosophical—my tiny

success would change nothing, I suspected; I'd still have to circumambulate the rug; I'd still have to live in my hole, surrounded, cowed—I went with Adam, Nina, and the cast to the Annex bar on Nassau Street, a watering hole for freethinkers on the prowl. Toasts were drunk, bubbles of flattery were blown, and I was pressed by the group to play the big shot, which was hard for me at first, but with a bit more alcohol and nicotine, alarmingly easy and instinctive. My speech sped up ferociously, my energized legs kicked away beneath the table, I rocked in my chair, I roared, I railed, I ripped. My paroxysm of pent-up ego drew people nearer—to feel the heat, perhaps—but eventually they withdrew to other groups, migrated to other scenes, and I found myself alone beside a stranger who looked like he'd slept in a field the night before but wore the vest-pocket pen of a professor. He'd plunked himself down at our table, uninvited, about an hour ago, and unobtrusively, stubbornly abided even though no one had spoken a word to him.

He introduced himself as Julian and said that it would be his privilege to buy me a cocktail in honor of my play. He said my work sounded interesting, provocative, judging by the talk around the table. A creep had cornered me, I feared. Still, because my throat was dry from boasting and I'd begun to dread leaving the bar, which meant either returning to the suite or going home with Nina to dish out sexual punishment till dawn, I accepted Julian's offer, clinked glasses with him, and asked him what he did.

The best conversation of my life ensued—one I could never have had in Minnesota and one that helped me forget my recent troubles by occupying me with cosmic issues of just the sort a place like Princeton should raise but so far hadn't, at least when I'd been listening. Julian taught psychology, he said, despite having no diploma in the subject, only a book he'd written as an amateur. It had grown out of his reading of ancient literature and concerned, he said, "the history of consciousness." I asked him to explain but keep it simple. He told me that he'd try. The modern human brain, he said, was actually two brains functioning as one brain, but there had been a time, long, long ago, when man's double brain had operated differently. Its parts, its halves, had been separate then, divided. In fact, they'd been virtual strangers to each other. When a thought arose in one of them, the other one, acting as a receiver, processed the thought as a voice, an actual voice. This voice seemed to come from outside the self, said Julian; it seemed to come from another being, really. But who was this being? Who were these secret speakers? Man had answered these questions in many ways. He'd conceived of gods and spirits, angels and demons, trolls and fairies. Muses.

"Back when, before the Breakdown," said Julian, "before the gods and voices fell silent, writers truly believed in inspiration. They experienced inspiration. It was real to them. Tell me: did you ever feel, during the composition of your script, that someone else, not you, was in control?"

"Honestly?"

"Of course."

"Honestly, I feel that way a lot. Down deep, in a quiet way, I feel it constantly. And sometimes it shakes me up a little. Should it?"

Julian shook his head, but not as vigorously as I would have liked.

"What was the 'Breakdown'?" I asked him. I had to know.

I had to know everything he did, suddenly. Julian was a genius, I'd decided, even if everything he'd said was crazy. And it probably was. Because I understood it.

"Ready?" said Nina, materializing behind me. She set her hands on my shoulders, squeezed them, kneaded. "You must be exhausted from your big night. I know I am. Let's hit the sheets."

"I'm kind of in the middle of something here."

Her fingers cooled and stiffened. "How much longer?"

"Awhile, maybe. I don't know."

Julian rose and slipped off to the men's room while I turned to Nina and managed a feat of candor that I'd been putting off for weeks, ever since I'd realized how bored I'd grown with the chore of besieging her in bed. I'd persisted because it offered me a break from the entrapment of my gloomy bunk, and also because being cherished as a brute, being adored as a gruesome primitive, beat being shunned by my roommates as a bum. But I wasn't a bum, I understood that night, and I didn't have to play a rapist.

"A little applause, and he craps all over us," was Nina's reaction to my breakup speech. "To be expected. Pitiful." At least she left the bar, though, trailing a mist of that acidic cat spray girls exude when they mean to fix you good.

Moments later Julian returned but he made no mention of the Breakdown. He was sweating and looked much drunker than before. He kept reaching a hand into his hair and scratching around as if hunting for a tick. Eventually he appeared to catch the thing, but when he unclasped his forefinger and thumb, gingerly, holding his hand out over the tablecloth so whatever it was would be visible if he dropped it, there was nothing to see.

"What changed in us?" I said, resolved to get him back on topic. "The half brains fused? They knit together? That's the opposite of a breakdown, isn't it? Are you saying that what we call insanity now, schizophrenia, was normal once?"

His face had gone as white and blank as the disk of frosting inside an Oreo. He drank back the rubble of ice and citrus peel remaining in his glass. He crunched and chewed. Finally he spoke, his last words of the night before he fetched his coat from under his chair and hung it, all crumpled and labels sticking up, on his drooping, slanted shoulders. "It gets too quiet when it gets late. I like it when it's loud, when there's commotion. That's how it should be. That's what we miss, I think. Our wonderful old noisy, friendly world."

My roommates were all on the sofa when I came in, watching a black-and-white movie, family style. Tim sat in the middle in his pj's holding a bowl of popcorn on his lap that everybody was digging in at once.

"Hey," said Jennifer, hearing me and turning. This was a thaw. Not much of one, but noticeable. Maybe the play had won me some respect.

"Hey there," I said. I slowed my steps. Tim looked back with bulging popcorn cheeks and awarded me a fleeting grin. Peter also cast a glance at me, then briefly lifted a finger of his left hand, which was hanging over the sofa back. My feet were angled toward the rug, but not acutely, not aggressively. Unless a more formal welcome was extended, I'd go no farther. It was up to them. An apology would be nice, too, though it needn't come immediately, just soon.

They faced the screen again, taking in the film, their temple muscles flexing as they munched.

"Good night," said Jennifer.

I mounted my bunk without undressing and glared at the ceiling, trying to blast a hole in it. In my play, the President was considering firing Polaris missiles so as to summon the Messiah. His aide, who'd been arguing for calm while dutifully pouring bourbon for the maniac, was standing behind the President's chair, in a perfect position to strangle him, when he picked up the phone to issue the directive. Stiffly, like a zombie, the aide raised his arms to perform his awful duty, but just as he was about to grip and squeeze, a battery of spotlights slashed the gloom with blinding beams of pure white light, causing both characters to jerk their heads back and behold . . . What exactly? We weren't shown. The lights were cut as abruptly as they'd been activated, all of the lights, and the theater went black. And perfectly silent. But was the action over? Not quite, it seemed. The void was too complete, too absolute. Somehow it would be ruptured.

But it wasn't. That was the dastardly Artaud in me. That was the radical new provocateur who'd killed off the bright, obliging Midwesterner and now masqueraded in his clothes. Snub them. Scorn them. Give them nothing. Give them only confusion, like they give you.

When my roommates went home to New York a few days later to get a jump on the Christmas holiday, I was left alone in the suite for eighteen hours, awaiting a flight I'd booked to Minnesota. I restrained myself at first, listening to one of Joshua's tapes of the late John Lennon. I'd become a snob by then, and the album I chose was obscure and difficult—the one that came out of his psychotherapy sessions, with all the grunting and shrieking about his parents. As darkness fell I grew agitated, though.

I found myself guzzling Moët & Chandon and standing in the middle of the rug, watching the network news on the TV. I was smoking a Camel. I let the ashes fall. Then I dropped the butt, still glowing, and ground it into the Persian rug with my heel. Ah, the odor of burning silk. I lit a fresh cigarette, drank off the champagne, uncorked another bottle from the mini-fridge, and walked around to the back of the TV, where I poured the wine through the ventilation slots in the plastic cabinet. As the liquid streamed over the hot internal circuitry, plumes of noxious vapor rose from the slots, through which I could see a sizzle of orange sparks and the occasional fat blue one. The blue ones popped like flashbulbs. They were gorgeous. On the screen, the picture shimmied, wobbled, then fractured into broad diagonal bands that thinned away and trembled down to nothing after another splash of wine.

After that I really got down to business. With a sturdy pair of scissors rummaged from Jennifer's antique vanity, I systematically clipped the harp of wires under the raised lid of Peter's Steinway. The instant I freed them from their tension, they sprang and curled away—an electrifying pleasure. I pounded the keys to make sure I'd killed the instrument. They made no sound and they stayed down. As a reprise, I cut the spokes and brake cables on Tim's ten-speed bike, which he'd left out in the hallway. I ravaged the tires, too, jabbing them with the open scissor blades. The tires' loss of air unbalanced the bike and it crashed over on its side. I stood on top of it like a trophy carcass and looked around for something else to wreck.

Adam peeked through the door about that time, his pupils gigantically dilated and glossy and slightly off center in his irises. I waved him in and opened more champagne. He knew the whole story of the rug and said it was no wonder I'd gone berserk, but he told me I'd gone too far with the piano. He seemed to harbor some notion that musical instruments were sacred or potently symbolic, the way some people think of books and artworks. I told him to come off it and be a friend. This seemed to wound him. To patch things up between us, he filled his mouth with champagne and swished his cheeks around, then spat a torrent of foam onto the sofa. "I just had a fun idea," I said. I pushed aside the curtains, opened the windows, and had Adam follow me outside to the snow-covered courtyard below the room. We packed our snowballs tight and threw them hard, attempting to clear the sills we couldn't see past. When we went in and took stock of the results—an off-kilter picture, a toppled lamp, heaps of gray slush on chair cushions and tables—Adam was seized by a fit of moral panic. He righted the fallen, mangled bicycle, he straightened up the picture, he rushed around kicking snow from the soaked rug. "Shit," he kept saying. "Oh shit oh god oh shit. This is so grotesquely fucked, Walt. Shit." He laid a flat hand on the mangled Steinway's lid and sorrowfully caressed the polished wood, then hung his head and collapsed onto the bench. He fingered some keys and they thudded dully, still dead.

"What's that nerve-gas smell?" he said. I directed his gaze to the TV, a dot of silver photons still pulsing in the middle of the screen. Its pesky persistence irked me. I speared it with a broom handle but the tip was too blunt and rounded for the job and bounced off the thick glass. Then I spied the ideal lance, a wrought-iron curtain rod with a finial of blade-shaped metal leaves. I stepped well back from my target to get a run at it and then impaled the thing. I ran it through, crushing the screen and leaving a length of rod protruding from the splintered cabinet. Adam groaned and covered his face. I told him he was excused. He staggered off, slipping and skidding in the melted snow.

In the morning I flew home to enjoy the winter holidays.

# Chapter Eight

Growing up, I'd respected authority, feared punishment, and played (or played *at* playing) by the rules, but at Princeton these habits and instincts weakened. I simply had no idea who ran the place. It allowed me to imagine no one did. The top officials were ghosts to me: a president I'd seen in photos but had never spotted in the flesh, a provost I'd heard about but wouldn't have recognized (what was a "provost," anyway?), and a number of deans who existed for me as signatures on documents which I seldom bothered to read. Nor were the first few professors I encountered particularly imposing figures. The younger ones struck me as squirrelly and insecure, while many of the tenured eminences seemed morose, distracted, and—when encountered outside the classroom—drunk.

Yet Princeton was orderly, orderly in the extreme, and I knew that this order had to come from somewhere. The grass was uniformly green, clipped right up to the edges of the sidewalks. The library books were in fine condition, generally, lined up straight and gapless on the shelves exactly where the catalogue said they'd be. The traditional a cappella groups who practiced their bumblebee-close harmonies in the resonant groins of Gothic archways were always maddeningly in tune. The black kids kept to their residential ghettos in down-campus Princeton Inn and Wilson colleges, while the Southern white guys, some of whom liked to hang Confederate flags from the ledges of their dorm-room windows, occupied the heights.

Even the outbursts of petty student anarchy felt orthodox and premeditated. One evening in December, Adam and I were passing Holder Hall, the neo-Gothic dormitory of choice for boozy, high-born sons of Dixie, when we heard a ruckus in its courtyard. Through an arch we saw dozens of naked bodies palely leaping and sprinting in the dusk. The bodies were smoothly muscled, sculptural, and though some of them had distinctly feminine voices, they appeared to be all male. Above them, in an open window, a pair of stereo speakers belched Southern rock.

"The Nude Olympics," Adam said. "Annual undergraduate student festival held at the first snowfall." He opened a palm to catch a meager flake.

"How come I've never heard of it?" I said.

"If you don't know about it, you don't belong at it."

The antiapartheid rallies on Cannon Green had a similar ritualistic air. For Joshua and other folk-guitar players, they seemed to constitute unofficial recitals. The protesters gathered around them in swaying circles, singing "This Land Is Your Land" with lowered eyes. Their block-print signs were always clean and neat and their bullhorn-amplified demands free of jarring language or obscenities. The security guards at their periphery affected relaxed, open stances that showed no fear of bloody scuffles or flying debris.

Maybe the source of order was the old buildings. That was my initial theory. Governance through architecture. Spires and high windows made people stand up straight. Stout granite walls promoted stout behavior.

The oldest of the buildings was Nassau Hall, which housed the office of the invisible president, who surely knew he was merely squatting there, surrounded by stones more influential than he was. A plain colonial structure of yellow masonry whose staircase was flanked by a pair of tarnished bronze tigers, the building had served as our nation's capitol once, back when we took our capitols less seriously, requiring only that they have bells on top and space to seat the Continental Congress, which wasn't much larger than a modern school board. The first time I beheld the edifice, through the dusty windshield of the taxi that carried me from the airport, I felt as though I'd completed a long swim back to my spawning grounds as an American. I had no desire to go inside, however. Nassau Hall didn't want me, I could feel it. The vault-like front doors. The tigers. Pass on by.

But once I grew used to dwelling among monuments, once I began to feel comfortable with grandeur, a certain lazy arrogance came over me. Princeton felt like a school without a principal where students were free to issue their own passes, police their own behavior, and grant their own pardons, if necessary. I concluded this was by design. For if, as the university asserted, we were indeed our nation's future leaders, then what better way to prepare us for the task of framing, interpreting, and defending its laws than letting us—on an experimental basis, in a relatively safe environment, supervised only by bell towers and tigers—operate as laws unto ourselves?

No wonder I felt entitled to sack the common room and take justice into my own hands: someday justice would end up in them anyway. Assuming, of course, that some hidden hand of power didn't reach down from the old towers and try to toss me out. I dismissed this possibility, though, because it had already happened, and I'd survived. It happened before John Lennon was gunned down, before the van from Bloomingdale's pulled up, while I was still finding my way around the campus, still hoping that the road of multiple choice had finally led me home.

"**M**r. Kirn?" I heard when I answered my dorm-room phone. "Is this Mr. Walter Kirn?"

"It is. I am."

The call came just after midterms, in the evening, when dire communications from officialdom are unexpected and unusually jarring. It served to inform me that I was under suspicion of violating the Princeton Honor Code, a solemn pledge of academic integrity that students were required to make in writing at the bottom of every test: "I pledge my honor that I have not violated the Honor Code during this examination." The caller didn't specify the nature of my alleged infraction, just summoned me to a room in Holder Hall at seven the next night. I asked for clarification. Holder Hall was a dormitory, I pointed out, not an administration building.

"The Honor Committee," the voice explained, "is entirely made up of other students."

"Other kids, you mean?"

"Your peers."

This sounded ominous, and not quite accurate. Any student

whose idea of fun, of bracing extracurricular amusement, was prosecuting and sentencing his classmates was certainly no peer of mine. Or were they drafted, these traitors? Were they conscripts? No, they had to be volunteers, these monsters—Goody Two-shoes who'd traded up to boots.

I didn't tell anyone where I was going the evening of the proceeding. I'd considered telling Joshua, but I wasn't sure if his Quaker passion for justice—so keen in the matter of black South Africa—extended to individuals. Nor could I guarantee him I was innocent. That would depend on the nature of the charges. I didn't remember ever actively cheating, but who really knew how cheating was defined here? I recalled being issued a booklet on the topic, but I'd treated it as junk mail.

"Walter or Walt? Or don't you have a preference? Fantastic to meet you. I'm Rob. Come right on in."

My inquisitor, my nemesis, the springy young Torquemada who'd answered the door, was a middleweight jock with a crushing, abusive handshake and the long hair of someone who favored short hair but hadn't been to the barber for a while. He pointed me to a dilapidated couch and went to fetch me a soda from a mini-fridge with several glasses stacked on top of it. His dorm room wasn't particularly fancy but it was the largest I'd ever seen. So this was how Princeton rewarded its quislings: with additional square footage.

I cast about for some reason to despise Rob as he brought me a cold drink and set a bowl of pretzel nuggets on the table between the sofa and his armchair. Once seated, he projected no majesty. His posture was loose and slumped. I noticed a cardboard folder on the table, but it seemed unimportant since he'd put the snack bowl on it.

"How were your midterms?" he asked me. "You survive?"

"Haven't heard yet. Hoping so." That I hadn't been read my rights yet troubled me. The trial might already be under way.

Rob reached for a nugget. "You transferred here?"

"I did."

"Hard to get in as a transfer student."

"Yes." But easy to get kicked out as one, I feared.

"If it feels like I'm beating around the bush, I'm sorry. This isn't a formal procedure, it's just an interview. It's just a conversation. A you-and-me thing." He ate his nugget and washed it down with a sip of beer. The can had been on the floor next to his chair and I'd thought it was empty, just trash. Incredible. They let the interrogators drink.

"So why did you cheat on your Spanish test last week?"

I protested. I denied. I took offense. I did so as a way of buying time for a mental review of the afternoon in question. I'd struggled and floundered, yes, but had I cheated? I recalled a moment of panic on page three when, aware that my time was running short, I'd glanced at the test sheets of the students beside me to determine how close they were to finishing. Perhaps I'd seen one of their answers—I didn't recall. Perhaps I'd borrowed this answer—I didn't recall. And now I had no incentive to recall. I picked up my Dr Pepper and switched my mind off before it could testify against itself.

"Forbidding cribbing and copying," said Rob, "is only *one* aspect of the Honor Code. It also requires students who witness cheating to report the infraction without delay. What I mean is, we've got a witness, Walt."

"Who?" I demanded. But I suspected I knew: Merrill, the Southern kid who'd sat across from me. He was fat in a way that suggested some imbalance, some inability to eliminate fluids, with a broad, soggy face and little seedlike eyes. He wore a coat and tie to class. We'd never actually argued, we'd never tangled, indeed we'd hardly spoken to each other, but we had sour chemistry from the day we met. A mystery. Some pairs of people are just natural adversaries.

"Not only is that irrelevant," said Rob, "it's also confidential."

"Not according to the Constitution. The right to face your accuser—"

"I know, I've heard. We get that old debating point a lot." Rob slid the folder from underneath the bowl and withdrew two sheets of paper. He laid them next to each other on the table, oriented so I could read them—copies of the Spanish test's fourth page covered in my jagged handwriting.

"Question twelve," said Rob. "You erased a wrong answer here, you'll notice, and wrote in the same one the girl beside you gave. That's awfully damning, I have to say. This thing will go quicker if you just admit it."

But would it go any better? I doubted it. The evidence, Rob was correct, seemed fairly grim, especially the apparent pressure I'd used in making the erasure; I'd almost rubbed right through the paper.

My righteous outrage turned to gloom. Where would I go after Princeton sent me packing? Cozy, forgiving Minnesota would have me because it had everyone, that was just its nature, but to me this would feel like crawling back into bed. My life would be like one long sick day. That left the mythic bus ride to New York City and the descent into Times Square degradation. Eventually, if the needle didn't take me, I might win the pity of a passing executive who'd give me a job in the basement of his headquarters refilling tape dispensers or sorting parcels. On my breaks I could write a novel or learn a language. It might turn out just fine. It might be how I should be living now, in fact.

"This totally blows for you, I'm sure," said Rob. "Maybe while I grab more Dr Pepper you could think about a statement. Show some remorse, why don't you? That never hurts. You want the same amount of ice?"

"I do."

My gaze drifted back to the test sheets as Rob walked off. By the time he got back he was facing Perry Mason. Some desperate survival instinct unleashed a latent gift for legal reasoning.

"Question twelve on test sheet four," I said, tapping a finger on exhibit A. "The critical word here—the one you say I stole—is 'sueño.' Is that agreed?"

Rob granted me nothing.

"And 'sueño' is the right answer, is it not?"

Silence. Rob infuriated me. The law was supposed to be blind, not deaf and dumb.

"It is indeed the right answer. And so is mine. Is it possible, Rob—and I submit it is; I submit it's even *likely*—that I arrived at this answer not through copying but in the same way my classmate did? Through *knowledge*?"

Rob pushed back all the way into his armchair, his face as rigid as a hieroglyph. In the Star Chamber of the Princeton Honor Committee, the sunlight of logic seldom shone, I gathered.

Rob parted his stony lips. "You looked around," he said. "Someone, our witness, saw you look around."

"I was checking my progress against my classmates'."

"You noticed the answer."

"To look is not to notice. To look is physical, not mental."

"But you erased what you'd already written."

"It's a crime to correct a mistake? To think again?"

"How do we know it was thinking, not copying?"

"You don't know. You *can't* know. Only I can, Rob."

His whole body perked up. "Then you admit it."

"What?" I asked.

"That you *know.*"

"I didn't say that. I said that I'm in a position to. You aren't."

"So *do* you?"

"Know?"

Rob nodded.

"It's possible. But why would I ever tell you?"

"The Honor Code."

"Versus the Fifth Amendment. Rock dulls scissors."

"Guilty or innocent? Yes or no," Rob said.

I ate a pretzel and let Rob's anger hang there. I thought he should have to feel it in the air. I thought it might force him to face his ugliness. Then I said, "I heard this from a senior. In France there's a critic, I forget his name, who teaches that antonyms, words that mean the opposite, don't really mean the opposite at all. They aren't the only alternatives, that is. There are other words between them. And all around them."

"Fascinating. Except this isn't France."

"You tell me to choose, but the words I'm meant to choose

from—'innocent,' 'guilty'—aren't my only choices. I choose another one. 'Unconvictable.'"

Rob pressed a thumb tip under the bony ridge between his eyebrows and just above his nose. He blew out a breath and let his head nod forward until the thumb tip held it like a hook. It looked like a stress-relief trick they taught to athletes.

"You can go. We're finished here," he said.

"For now or forever?"

"I have to speak to people."

"I'm sorry I got prickly. What I'd wish you'd admit is I shouldn't *have* to choose. Not 'innocent,' not 'guilty,' not anything. I shouldn't be in this position. You have no *case*."

Rob thumbed his brow as I stood up from the couch. I pitied him, suddenly. He'd surely been cajoled into this job, and now, having realized he wasn't really up to it—and having taken for granted the spacious dorm room, which had seemed at the time like such a prize—he probably wanted to murder the smooth talker who'd recruited him.

"I'm very sorry we met this way," I said.

"How else would we have met?" said Rob. An excellent point. We came from different tribes. And now I knew to avoid his, to not go near it, the same way I gave a wide berth to Nassau Hall and, not long afterward, to the Persian rug.

The fear of a terrible reckoning, of expulsion, of banishment from the ninety-ninth percentile and a quick trip to whatever hell is reserved for fallen overachievers who've mastered or outmaneuvered every challenge except adjusting to the company of their own merciless species, hit me on the last day of Christmas break, on the way to the airport in my father's car. I belched sour orange juice into my throat as I remembered the limp piano wires, the toxic odor of the frying Sony, the glorious, heedless manic rush of tearing apart my prison with my bare hands. With motive galore and sole access to the crime scene, how had I expected to get away with it? I hadn't, obviously. This seemed to mean that I'd been courting punishment, soliciting some absolute rejection that would remove the tension of awaiting one. I didn't buy it, though. The better explanation, I believed, was rooted in Julian's theories about consciousness, at least as I'd been able to understand them. We humans had come to believe over the centuries that our thoughts and actions belonged to us, that they were wholly ours, from our own skulls, and that had led us to feel we could control them or, when we couldn't, that we should answer for them. But maybe it wasn't true. Maybe, at times, the mind slipped back, evolution and history reversed themselves, and the ancient phantoms regained command.

My defense, if it ever came to mounting one, would be possession, I decided. Or regression, that is. And it might just be the truth. A throwback lobe had made me slay the Steinway.

My father exited the freeway and took a shortcut through downtown St. Paul that was only a shortcut under ideal conditions. As usual, they didn't obtain today. There was construction. Then there was an accident. Luckily, we'd set out early, so being late for my flight was not our worry. Our worry—not just mine, I knew—was having extra time to talk but nothing much to say.

"So it's been good? You're getting used to it?" My father had asked the same thing at Christmas dinner and I'd answered the same way I did now.

"It's different. It's a different kind of place."

"I can't disagree. And it's tough sometimes, I bet. But I made the best friends of my life at that damned place and you will, too, if you make a little effort."

I didn't respond. Too anxious. And now too sad. I'd met my father's wondrous college friends—all three or four of them—though only briefly, and never more than twice. They lived spread out around the country, mostly in the East, and every few years one would pass through Minnesota and show up at our dinner table, where my brother and I were expected to receive them like long-lost relatives. They always got drunk before the meal was over. Often, they arrived drunk. Then they told stories about getting drunk. For a few days after they left my father would talk about how much he missed them, how much they meant to him, what fine guys they were, but then a year would go by without him mentioning them, except when he was drunk.

By the time we cleared the congestion and delays I was wondering if I should go back to school at all. I might be arrested on arrival. I'd certainly be given another bill; a fantastically large bill that I couldn't duck and that my father would learn about eventually, possibly from a judge, who'd make him pay it. I considered confessing in the car to him; we still had fifteen minutes before the airport. I studied his profile, trying to gauge his mood—his character, really—and guess how he'd respond. He was dressed for work in an old suit bought from a thrift store called Next to New. Refusing to pay full price for office wear was part of his rebellion against the business world, as was his fondness for Copenhagen snuff. He spat a big gob of it out his rolled-down window and the subzero January air instantly froze it in a fan shape on the backseat window behind his shoulders.

"You know how you say about 3M sometimes that they discourage being your own man?"

"I guess I've said that. Or felt that. Sometimes. Why?"

"Princeton can be like that, too."

"I'm sure it can be. That's just the world for you, isn't it?" he said.

He craned his neck, merging back onto the freeway, and shot into a gap between two trucks. The daredevil move convinced me to stop talking. Instead of listening, he'd been gauging road speeds. I think he wanted me to know it, too. I think he was trying on purpose to cut me short. Desolation was rolling off me in waves and he wasn't stupid; he sensed I had bad news. He'd probably sensed it since I'd gotten home. But bad news from me angered him, I'd always felt. It might require him to perform some duty, and duty, to my father, always meant loss of freedom, never an opportunity for strength.

I knew this because I thought the same way.

"Welcome, welcome, welcome," said Jennifer.

She was alone on the sofa drinking tea and leafing through a magazine. The common room had been restored. The TV was turned on, the rug looked clean and sleek, and on the piano was a sheet of music and Peter's ashtray, bristling with butts. A Christmas miracle. And ominous.

"How was your break?"

I shrugged. My throat had closed.

"Mine was perfect. Just heavenly," she said.

I smiled, re-smiled, dipped my head, and pushed down the hall against a current of dread. Each step took the energy of a hundred steps, the surge against me was that strong, but I told myself that if I made it to the bedroom, where I could hear Joshua singing "Heart of Gold," I could plead with the Lord to turn back time.

"You do know you're going to jail," said Jennifer before I'd gotten very far. "My father's lawyers will see to it. You're toast."

I stayed in my bunk for thirty-six hours, feigning the flu and subsisting on buttered dinner rolls that Joshua brought wrapped in napkins from the dining hall and set on my desk while I coughed and hacked and shivered. He allowed me a full day of drama before explaining, in his calm yet disquieting Quaker way, that my roommates were serious indeed about pursuing criminal charges but might be persuaded to show leniency if I made restitution and showed remorse.

"For what?" I croaked.

"I'm just saying. I'm not judging. I'm not conveying any assumptions."

"So what are you saying?"

"Make sure to eat."

Adam came by later in the day and, in return for my promise not to squeal on him, left me a joint he'd dipped in liquid cocaine. When I lit up after he left, a crow with a scrap of something pink and fleshy dangling from its horrid black beak landed on the ledge outside my window, fluffed its feathers, and started pacing. It seemed to expect me to let it in the room. I willed myself into unconsciousness. Nina was next to my bunk when I woke up but the crow was gone. I suspected a metamorphosis. Confirmation came when she produced a packet of effervescent vitamin powder that she ripped open with her teeth, drizzled into a glass of lukewarm water, and presented to me like a witch's potion, still bubbling.

"First you're going to shower and brush your teeth. Then we're going to a play," she said. "And no, they're not out there. The coast is clear."

But my nightmare continued in the theater. Student actors whose heads were wrapped in bandages and whose faces were covered with fake boils crawled and limped and writhed across the stage. Baby powder used to gray their hair came off in clouds and drifted through the lights. The set conjured up no specific place or period and had to be explained to me by Nina. It was a French insane asylum, she said, during the era of revolution. The script combined verse and screaming. Its meaning escaped me. When the actors flooded into the audience, snorting and cackling and spitting, I formed a grudge against the art of live performance itself. It seemed unfair that I couldn't attack them back.

At the Annex after the show I drank as much liquor as Nina had money for and let her discourse about Artaud and "the sickness," whose nature she didn't specify but which had been bred by society, not people. I failed to see the distinction—people *were* society. Nina treated my observation as a witticism rather than a point to be debated and I let it pass. It was frivolous, under the circumstances. The circumstances being my looming trial for felonious destruction of property. No date for it had been set, but it would come.

"Don't be silly. Don't be histrionic. Their insurance covered the damage. All they want is an apology. And make it spectacular. Bended-knee stuff. Really."

"I didn't do it."

"Please."

"It must have been an intruder."

"This hurts to watch."

"This hurts to be seen doing."

"You have problems."

"Problems you must like," I said. "May I ask you why?"

"I'm sure you know."

"I truly don't. I want to, though. Maybe then I'll like them, too. Right now I hate them. Tell me."

"Doomed is sexy. Lost is a turn-on in cute smart boys. Come over to my house. You can play intruder."

I didn't want to, but I did her bidding. I knew better, but I heeded her. As though she were not a girl I could put off, a human being I could disappoint, but an irresistible spirit from my own brain.

The next day my phone rang. Nassau Hall. Or maybe it was an immaterial aide in the ethereal office of the provost. Or some dean who slept in a coffin in a closet infested with bats and spiderwebs. In Princeton's neo-Gothic shadowland, the figures who spoke from the castle were all one ghost.

The voice didn't let me get a word in edgewise. It ordered me to gather up my things and move to a university-owned house a block away from campus. The voice provided an address and a room number as well as instructions on obtaining a door key. No discussion. Go immediately. Without saying so directly, the voice suggested that my prompt obedience would close the file on my vandalism. I hung up feeling relieved but mystified. Had justice been served, evaded, or postponed? I couldn't imagine through what process, or on the basis of what evidence, what testimony, what arguments, my case had been adjudicated. I further feared that I'd incurred some debt, some burdensome institutional obligation. Was this how Princeton sucked students into the Honor Committee?

Joshua came in while I was packing but didn't inquire about my destination, just offered to help me fold my shirts and sweaters. His beatific detachment would be missed. He expected so little from me. He accepted so little. Whole weeks had passed when I'd hardly acknowledged his presence, had barely checked for his presence in the room, and yet, I realized now, he'd been there beside me almost the whole time. Mourning John Lennon. Playing hits from *Godspell*. Growing his beard in a corner.

"It's fine," I said. "They're making me move off campus, but it's fine."

"Where off campus?"

I gave the house's address.

"Lots of committed vegetarians there. They all pitch in in the kitchen. You might like that."

"If a space opens up," I said, "you could move there, too. I'd like that."

He crossed the arms of my homely flannel shirt and neatly reduced it to a square that he set on top of the garments I'd folded myself. His packing skills put mine to shame. I clamped the suitcase between my knees, compressed it, latched it, and hoisted it off the floor. It was heavy with books that I'd vowed to read, not skim. I wanted to reform.

Going out, I said, "I'm curious. How do Quakers pray?"

"Why?" Joshua asked.

"I heard you do it differently. Than Mormons, say."

"How do Mormons pray?"

"The usual. 'Please' and 'thank you' and 'amen.'"

"We sit very still, in silence, and we listen."

"Listen for what?"

"Whatever comes."

"Interesting. Does it matter where it comes from?"

He cocked his head. "Not sure I get you there."

"I'm not sure I do, either."

In the common room, at the resurrected piano, Jennifer, Tim, and Peter were working on songs for an original musical Peter hoped to mount later in the semester. "Break a leg," I said, going by. I meant it. But then, at the door, I regretted meaning it. I took a Quaker breath. "Break a leg," I said again, but nicely. They didn't look over at me. Their backs stayed turned.

I slammed the door hard enough to crack the casement and pounded down the stairs into the cold.

I VOWED TO GET SERIOUS ABOUT MY STUDIES. I CHOSE TO major in English, since it sounded like something I might already know. I assumed that my classmates and I would study the classics and analyze their major themes and such, but instead we were buffeted with talk of "theory," whatever that was. The basic meanings of the poems, short stories, and essays contained in the hefty Norton anthologies that anchored our entry-level reading lists were treated by certain professors as trivial, almost beneath discussion; what mattered, we were given to understand, were our "critical assumptions."

I, for one, wasn't aware of having any. Until I was sixteen or so, my only reading had consisted of Hardy Boys mysteries, world almanacs, books on UFOs, a Time-Life history of World War II, and a handful of pulpy best sellers linked to movies (*The Day of the Jackal* and *The Exorcist* stood out), which I'd read for their sex scenes and air of general perversity. I knew a few great authors' names from scanning dust jackets in the public library and watching the better TV quiz shows, but the only serious novels I'd ever cracked were *Frankenstein, Moby-Dick* (both sold to me by crafty high-school teachers as gripping tales of adventure, which they weren't), and *The Great Gatsby* by Fitzgerald. *Gatsby* I actually finished. Among my mother's collection of mail-order leatherette masterpieces, it was the shortest, the least remote in time, and the only one narrated by a Minnesotan. The tale didn't strike me as tragic or cautionary. To me, it was the invigorating chronicle of several high-spirited Midwesterners storming through the mansions of the East. Gatsby's demise barely registered for me. I focused on the dancing and the drinking, the motorcar outings, the rich girls, the grand hotels.

With virtually no stored literary material about which to harbor critical assumptions, I relied on my gift for mimicking authority figures and playing back to them their own ideas as though they were conclusions I'd reached myself. I'd honed these skills on the speech team back in high school, and I didn't regard them as sins against the Honor Code. Indeed, they embodied an honor code: my own. "Be Honored," it stated. "Or Be Damned." To me, imitation and education were different words for the same thing, anyway. What was learning but a form of borrowing? And what was intelligence but borrowing slyly?

In my private Princeton honors program, the deployment of key words was crucial, just as the recognition of them had been on the SAT. Because I despaired of ever grasping these theory words, style of presentation was everything. "Liminal," spoken breezily enough, and "valuational," served up with verve, could make a professor shiver and drop his chalk, but if delivered hesitantly, they bombed. They bombed before they reached one's lips, while still emerging from one's throat. Unless they were spit out promptly and with spirit, such words could actually choke a person.

This suffocating sensation often came over me whenever I opened *Deconstruction and Criticism*, a collection of essays by leading theory people that I spotted everywhere that year and knew to be one of the richest sources around for words that could turn a modest midterm essay into an A-plus tour de force. Here is a sentence (or what I took to be one because it ended with a period) from the contribution by the Frenchman Jacques Derrida, the volume's most prestigious name: "He speaks his mother tongue as the language of the other and deprives himself of all reappropriation, all specularization in it." On the same page I encountered the windpipe-blocking "heteronomous" and "invagination." When I turned the page I came across— stuck in a footnote—"unreadability."

That word I understood, of course.

But real understanding was rare with theory. It couldn't be depended on at all. Boldness of execution was what scored points. With one of my professors, a snappy "heuristic" usually did the trick. With another, the charm was a casual "praxis." Even when a poem or story fundamentally escaped me, I found that I could save face with terminology, as when I referred to T. S. Eliot's *The Waste Land* as "semiotically unstable." By this I meant "hard." All the theory words meant "hard" to me, from "hermeneutical" to "gestural." Once in a while I'd look one up and see that it had a more specific meaning, but later—sometimes only minutes later—the definition would catch a sort of breeze, float away like a dandelion seed, and the word would go back to meaning "hard."

The need to finesse my ignorance through such trickery— honorable trickery to my mind, but not to other minds, perhaps—left me feeling hollow and vaguely haunted. Seeking security in numbers, I sought out the company of other frauds. We recognized one another instantly. We toted around books by Roland Barthes, Hans-Georg Gadamer, and Walter Benjamin. We spoke of "playfulness" and "textuality" and concluded before we'd read even a hundredth of it that the Western canon was "illegitimate," a veiled expression of powerful group interests that it was our duty to subvert. In our rush to adopt the latest attitudes and please the younger and hipper of our instructors—the ones who drank with us at the Nassau Street bars and played the Clash on the tape decks of their Toyotas as their hands crept up our pants and skirts—we skipped straight from ignorance to revisionism, deconstructing a body of literary knowledge that we'd never constructed in the first place.

For true believers, the goal of theory seemed to be the lifting of a great weight from the shoulders of civilization. This weight was the illusion that it was civilized. The weight had been set there by a range of perpetrators—members of certain favored races, males, property owners, the church, the literate, natives of the northern hemisphere—who, when taken together, it seemed to me, represented a considerable portion of everyone who had ever lived. Then again, of course I'd think that way. Of course I'd be cynical. I was one of them.

So why didn't I feel like one of them, particularly just then? Why did I, a member of the classes that had supposedly placed the weight on others and was now attempting to redress this crime, feel so crushingly weighed down myself?

I wasn't one of theory's true believers. I was a confused young opportunist trying to turn his confusion to his advantage by sucking up to scholars of confusion. The literary works they prized—the ones best suited to their project of refining and hallowing confusion—were, quite naturally, knotty and oblique. The poems of Wallace Stevens, for example. My classmates and I found them maddeningly elusive, like collections of backward answers to hidden riddles, but luckily we could say "recursive" by then. We could say "incommensurable."

Both words meant "hard."

I grew to suspect that certain professors were on to us, and I wondered if they, too, were fakes. In classroom discussions, and even when grading essays, they seemed to favor us over the hard workers, whose patient, sedentary study habits, and sense that confusion was something to be avoided rather than celebrated, appeared unsuited to the new attitude of antic postmodernism that I had mastered almost without effort. To thinkers of this school, great literature was an incoherent con, and I—a born con man who knew little about great literature—had every reason to agree with them. In the land of nonreadability, the nonreader was king, it seemed. Long live the king.

This lucky convergence of academic fashion and my illiteracy emboldened me socially. It convinced me I had a place at Princeton after all. I hadn't chosen it, exactly, but I'd be foolish not to occupy it. Otherwise I'd be alone.

Finally, without reservations or regrets, I settled into the ranks of Princeton's Joy Division—my name for the crowd of moody avant-gardists who hung around the smaller campus theaters discussing, enjoying, and dramatizing confusion. One of their productions, which I assisted with, required the audience to contemplate a stage decorated with nothing but potted plants. *Plants and Waiters*, it was called. My friends and I stood snickering in the wings making bets on how long it would take for people to leave. They, the "waiters," proved true to form. They fidgeted but they didn't flee. Hilarious.

And, for me, profoundly enlightening. Who knew that serious art could be like this? Who would have guessed that the essence of high culture would turn out to be teasing the poor saps that still believed in it? Certainly no one back in Minnesota. Well, the joke was on them, and I was in on it. I could never go back there now. It bothered me that I'd ever even lived there, knowing that people here on the great coast (people like me—the new, emerging me) had been laughing at us all along. But what troubled me more was the dawning realization that had I not reached Princeton, I might never have discovered this; I might have stayed a rube forever. This idea transformed my basic loyalties. I decided that it was time to leave behind the sort of folks whom I'd been raised around and stand—for better or for worse—with the characters who'd clued me in.

I soaked lentil beans in iron stew pots, formed falafel patties in my bare hands, harvested bean sprouts with pinking shears, and squeezed the moisture from slices of tofu between double layers of paper towels. My new housemates, all upperclassmen and Grateful Dead fans, believed that preparing and consuming food were sacramental acts. The kitchen was a temple, and the mood at our table was reverential. There, according to our leader, Greg, a bearded political science major with mesmerizing, unfocused brown eyes and sandal-strap tan lines on his feet, we "shared the good things of the earth."

Among these good things were the hallucinogenic mushrooms that Greg must have had some nearby source for, because they were moist when he shook them from their bags. Sometimes he shook them directly into the soup pot. Due to his knowledge of life in poorer countries and to his sympathy for their customs and folkways and religions, Greg thought of himself as a sort of village shaman. This gave him a lot of leeway in his conduct. One weekend I caught him sleeping with a girl who'd flown out to visit me from Macalester College. Instead of apologizing or scurrying off, he looked up from the bed—my bed—and said, "In some cultures, Walter, men share their women proudly." Then, to my girl, whose head was under a pillow, he said, "It's okay. Stay mellow. I expected this. At some stage when you trip on shrooms, there's always a visitation from the shame realm."

There is no drug scene like an Ivy League drug scene. Kids can't just get high; they have to seek epiphanies. They have to ground their mischief in manifestos. The most popular one around the veggie house held that drugs, especially psychedelic drugs—especially plant-based psychedelic drugs—helped to break down the rigid inner partitions that restricted one's full humanity. This belief in creative derangement came down to us from Baudelaire, Rimbaud, and the Beat poets, but in my case it didn't quite apply because my mind had few partitions in the first place. It was one big dark and empty room with scraps of paper strewn all over the floor.

Our drug sessions were the opposite of parties; they brought on bouts of crushing introspection and spirals of anxious cerebration. One night Adam came over to the house for Thai spicy noodles and a square of blotter acid. After the bowls and chopsticks were put away, the smells of burned sesame oil and peanut butter and the climate of well-fed hippie piety drove us outside for a long walk. Our first stop was the Princeton chapel, which was closer in size and splendor to a cathedral. Something had drawn us there. As we walked down its infinite main aisle toward the gaudy holy end, Adam dropped to the floor—not kneeling, sprawling. He said an invisible force had knocked him down. He said it seemed to be displeased with us. We scrambled out of the place as though pursued and hid behind a sculpture by Picasso of a gigantic triangular-faced woman. It, too, had an angry force field, though. It, too, cast us away.

"I feel punished," said Adam as we wandered. "I feel like I offended. Did I offend?"

"Don't let those thoughts push in."

"They're in. They're here."

"I know," I said quietly. "Me, too."

"But you didn't quit premed," said Adam. "You didn't renounce tradition and leave the path."

"Maybe I was never on the path."

"You had to be. You're here."

We ended up on the grounds of the Institute for Advanced Studies, a lofty think tank secluded in the woods. The place was best known as a haven for famous physicists, including Albert Einstein and Niels Bohr, and through its lamplit windows we glimpsed the silhouettes of Nobel Prize winners, their heads surrounded by pulsing pink coronas that persisted even when we blinked. Now and then someone would pass us in the darkness, absorbed, we imagined, in algebraic reveries related to fusion reactors and plasma beams.

Toward midnight we sat down under a tree—a benevolent presence that seemed to offer shelter from the sinister brilliance all around us—and reached the conclusion that Princeton was a portal for arrogant, Luciferian energies bent on the overthrow of God and Nature. It was a well-disguised weapons plant. An armory. The reason the chapel had repelled us was to prevent us from gazing upon its altar, which was probably dressed with a cross inside an atom. We decided to purify ourselves. We scooped up clods of mud and grass, smeared them all over our arms and throats and cheeks, and danced like druids, like dervishes. The idea was to whirl back to a time before telescopes and written alphabets. Loving presences would surely welcome us. They'd dress us in robes of softest spider silk and take us to meet the others who'd returned. Their numbers would astonish us.

Our behavior attracted attention from a guard whose flashlight beam swarmed with photons the size of snowflakes. He asked us what we were doing. We tried to tell him. The guard seemed kind; not a guard at all—a guardian. He aimed his cone of fluffy radiance in a direction that struck us as the true one. We thanked him, he nodded, and we set out.

"Back from your journeys," said a bearded figure when, by a route impossible to map, we finally arrived in paradise.

His name was Greg, we learned.

He made us soup.


Other trips ended badly.

A self-proclaimed Marxist from New York City and part of the Joy Division crowd, Barry Lehrer was the only child of a classics professor and a nightclub singer. When we met, he'd just returned to Princeton from a one-year suspension for some infraction he claimed to be innocent of but wouldn't talk about. I assumed it had to do with drugs. He wore his shirts unbuttoned to the breastbone, not to display his unimpressive chest but for the same reason he rarely flushed a toilet, wiped his shoes before entering a building, or pulled a door completely shut: his philosophical hostility to social niceties and common courtesies. They were forms of unpaid labor, he felt, which propped up a system destined for collapse.

"Everything's labor. *Everything*," said Barry. We were sitting up late in my bedroom at the veggie house smoking pot and talking socialism. "Waiting for green before you cross is labor."

"What's wrong with labor?"

"Nothing. Labor's noble. Unless it's coerced, converted into capital, and used to manufacture the very chains"—he held his wrists together in front of him and mimed a failed attempt to separate them—"that bind us from the hour of our birth."

"The only reason I wait for the green light is so I don't get run over by a car."

"It's an act of submission. Face it."

"That's extreme."

"I hold to a pretty high standard, I realize that." He reached for the milk-crate bookshelf beside my bed and extracted what was, at the moment, my favorite book: an anthology of American poetry put out by a major textbook publisher.

"Can you believe this corporate perversion? Wake up, Walt Whitman, you're a commodity. Get with it, Emily Dickinson, you've been marketed." He opened the book and flipped through its thin pages—I heard their fragile corners tearing—and read from a poem whose title I couldn't see. "*America why are your libraries full of tears? America when will you send your eggs to India?*"

"Who is that? I like it."

"Don't get stuck on authorship."

"Tell me. Show me."

Barry closed the book.

A few days later he pulled up to the house in a compact car with mismatched tires. He looked to be on the fourth day of his labor-saving five-day shaving cycle. He invited me on an outing to New York to buy some cocaine from a "batshit party girl" whom he said he'd gone to high school with. He instructed me to bring cigarettes and cash. I had a little money for a change because I'd just cashed my first paycheck from my new job bartending at the Princeton faculty club. He jammed the bills I gave him in his back pocket and asked me if I was holding out on him. I was honest. "Yes," I said. "I kept a few bucks for myself, if that's okay." He proceeded to lecture me on why it wasn't, battering me with quotes from Marx. He even disputed the legitimacy of the term "myself." He broke me down. My last twenty was transferred to his trousers, where it had belonged all along, supposedly.

We drove to the Engineering Quad and picked up Barry's friend, Jason, a pale computer whiz with all the characteristics of a bad stutterer except for the stutter itself. We shot down Route 1 past motels and pancake houses, entered a tunnel tiled like a bathroom, and emerged onto a downtown street full of police cars and the types they shadow. I'd been to Manhattan three or four times before, but always with Nina, to see plays, so all I knew of the city was Times Square and the plaza of Lincoln Center. From these visits I'd formed the impression that New York was largely populated by middle-aged couples who didn't get along well and went to shows so they wouldn't have to speak.

This excursion was different; I got to look around. I saw that, in fact, most New Yorkers were lonely pedestrians preoccupied by their reflections in store windows. What also struck me, quite pleasantly, were the city's angles, cuts, and edges—its thrilling, un-Midwestern jaggedness. I also liked its hollowness, which announced itself when our car drove over manholes, rattling their iron lids, and again when I poured the dregs of a papaya drink over a grating we were standing on and watched the liquid drip down into the gloom. How high the city stretched was plain to see, but I hadn't appreciated how deep it went.

The elevator to the girl's apartment—her parents' place, Barry told me on our zoom up—let us out not in a hallway but in the middle of a living room. Its chief architectural feature was a long sheath of spotless floor-to-ceiling glass that aroused my suicidal side by seeming to promise an endless plunge through ecstasies of light. The rooftop of the nearest building was at least ten floors below us, its surface littered with sheets of paper (newspaper?) that seemed to have been deposited there by some unfathomable updraft from the streets.

"Bizarre perspective, isn't it?" said Jason, joining me at my observation post behind an L-shaped leather sofa. He'd just emerged from the girl's bedroom, where he and Barry had gone to wake her up. I got the sense it was usual with her to be in bed at nine p.m.

"It just seems strange to me," said Jason, "that we can look down on it this way. Shouldn't it be the highest thing around?"

"Shouldn't what?"

"The UN. That's UN headquarters."

Jason held a knife blade under my nose and I snorted pow-dered cocaine for the first time. I felt nothing, absolutely normal, until our hostess, our connection, Holly, materialized at my side in a white bathrobe and pressed a bottle of beer into my hand. The chill of the moisture-beaded glass was the purest cold I'd ever felt, an elemental condition, not just a temperature. Holly's skin seemed elemental, too. The front of her robe was open, open wide, exposing all that she offered as a female, from her col-larbone on down. I'd never seen such a swath of softness. It was skin that might have been cultured in a lab or harvested, through some blasphemous new process, from the wrists of infants.

"You're Howard?" she asked me. The crust that rimmed her nostrils was like salt on a margarita glass.

"Walter."

"That's mostly a black name nowadays."

"Really?"

"Like Luther. Don't take that wrong or anything."

"So how should I take it?"

"To mean you have a big one. Or that I hope you do," she said.

Barry proposed an outing to a jazz bar that featured a no-table combo on Friday nights. He pressed the plan with fervor, naming the players and the greats they'd played with, hinting that some were ill and might not live long, and hinting, too, that the combo might break up soon. It would probably be our last chance to hear these legends, but we had to leave now to get a table, he said. I thought I knew his game. His aim was to get Holly out in public where we could share her. He'd noticed how much she liked me.

She didn't want to go. "Everyone says it's the great American art form, but I think jazz just makes it hard to talk. Even if you can hear each other over it, you're meant to pay all this attention to the performances. Like they're magic or something. Blow, man, blow. I hate it."

Barry fought her. Barry won. His argument wasn't explicitly based on Marxism, but it did exploit notions of guilt and obligation that a non-Marxist wouldn't have thought to use. At the club, we were shown to a table by the stage and fawned on by a desperate waiter. The place wasn't empty but it wasn't mobbed, and the players looked healthy and solidly united. I was so buzzed I forgot to drink my drink, but then I remembered and couldn't get served fast enough. Holly's behavior was disengaged. She rose from the table in the middle of solos and drifted around the room, smoking and peering down into her glass. The only person she spoke to was poor Jason—about computers, of all things. He seemed unused to attention from pretty girls and shut his eyes as though protecting himself whenever she leaned in close.

Barry gave in. We drove back to Holly's building. She rolled her eyes at the doorman, which I interpreted as her way of telling someone who knew her well that, once again, she'd been forced to take the reins back from people who'd promised her a night of fun but hadn't delivered, same as always. He tipped his cap as if to say: good job.

Next, we got involved with makeup. I sat on a stool in the converging beams of several recessed ceiling lights as Holly dragged a stick of eyeliner across the tender edges of my lids. She liked making guys look androgynous, she said, but they had to have high cheekbones, and mine were gorgeous. She chose a rich, cigar-colored mascara which she said matched "the under tint" of my complexion, but when she leaned back to scrutinize the job, she seemed unimpressed by the effect, so she covered the brown with a sparkly purple-green. Next she concentrated on my lips, seeking "a Cheshire cat effect." She adored it, declaring it a masterpiece, and forced me, physically forced me, with both hands, to turn my obstinate head to face the mirror.

"You're not half bad at the glam look. You pull it off." She found a music magazine and held up a photo of David Bowie next to my face for comparison's sake. It stunned me to see she was right, that this mode suited me.

"Is any of Barry's coke left? I haven't done any lately. He keeps avoiding me."

"The only coke tonight, as far as I know, is mine," said Holly. "I thought he slipped you some."

I shook my head. "And I'm the one who gave him money to buy it."

"No one bought anything. You didn't hear me. I share my dangerous narcotics. Free. Barry!"

"Don't."

"He conned you. You're his friend. Barry, get in here, you greedy traitor Jew!"

"Holly—"

"I'm a Jew, too. I have the right."

But Barry couldn't be called to task, I learned. His radar for others' displeasure was too keen. He knew instinctively when the game was up and when to make himself unavailable. He'd probably run to the deli for cigarettes.

"If Truman weren't sick in bed upstairs, I'd ask him down to hang out with us," said Holly. "Barry says you're an author."

"I wrote one play."

"I'll call upstairs anyway. He might be better. Truman's the best. You should meet him. He's a blast."

I shifted without warning in my chair and Holly's pencil skittered down my chin. I knew some things about this Truman fellow. My mother had befriended him at the exclusive, lakeside rehab clinic where she'd night-nursed during my high-school years. "Truman said something interesting last night. We were drinking decaf at my station. I mentioned you. Your vocabulary. Your grades. I told him you might want to be a writer. He said, 'Millie, your precious little boy is either a writer or he isn't.' So I said, 'How will he know if he's a writer?' And Truman, my little Martian, he shook his head, his dear little head, and said, 'If he keeps on doing it.'"

"Let's not bother the guy," I said to Holly.

"Truman loves to party. He won't be bothered."

"I've heard that maybe he needs to take it easy."

"You're what now, his doctor? His psychiatrist? I'll bet he's all by himself up there tonight."

"Then he'll probably want to spend it writing."

"You don't know many writers," Holly said.

We went out again, I wasn't sure why, and over the next three hours or so the night turned into what I'd learn to call, once I'd spent more time in New York City, "one of those." Just one of those. There was an ashtray full of bloody napkins, a limping pigeon with no beak, two convincing sightings of Andy Warhol twenty minutes and thirty blocks apart, and a woman taxi driver who read fortunes by gazing deep into her rearview mirror. Later on, when the coke was running out, there was a stairwell whose stairs went so far down I couldn't believe we'd ever climbed them. They also went so far up that I quit trying.

I decided this was symbolic in some fashion, perhaps the basis for another play. Feeling trapped and short of breath, I opened a steel door beside the stairwell and was confronted with a storage area for what looked to be at least one hundred heavy-duty upright vacuums. They were lined up like tanks about to enter battle, their red dust bags suggestive of pent-up fury. They radiated hegemony and praxis, ambiguity and hermeneutics. They were a text, but one I found unreadable.

I heaved the vault-like door shut until it latched.

"How far did they have to go to find a store?" I said, speaking directly into Holly's left ear. I was lying on top of her, on her bony back, in a bedroom from which I could see a distant bridge packed with stationary cars. Which rush hour was it? Wasn't it the weekend? A helicopter hammered past the window on a warlike upward vector. Barry and Jason had been gone for hours.

"Roll off or have at me," Holly said. "Wait, though. I need fluids." She wriggled free and left me in the room gazing into her enormous closet at a long regression of what appeared to be identical black dresses. She gave me a wine cooler when she got back, but it was too pink to drink, too sickly sweet. "If you're nervous about getting back to school," she said, "we'll call the garage and have my Jag sent over. Its oil cakes up when it just sits."

But I wasn't nervous about returning. What worried me was leaving. Above me, Truman Capote with the flu, below me the General Assembly of the UN, and off to the side—to every side—figures whom I might never meet again. Not that I'd met them this time. But I might have. Movers and shakers, living, working, suffering, inhabiting their fame. The only reason to return to Princeton was to equip myself to come back here.

"What do your parents do?" I asked.

"My stepmom primarily just beautifies. Beautifies and goes on pilgrimages. The kind where you chant and drink yak milk and sleep with monks. That's basically beautifying, too, but she calls it 'peace work.' I'm cool with it. It's fine. Of course, if she dies in a bus crash in Bhutan, I wouldn't mind that, either. I hope she will."

"What does your father do to support all this?"

"All this what?" Holly asked me.

"This life," I said.

"Art. He's in art."

"That's all? Just art?"

"For now."

This news encouraged me. I was only a sophomore; I could still switch majors. I could still learn to paint and cast bronze sculptures. Then again, Truman, whose apartment was probably just like this one, authored novels—and not particularly long ones, either, to judge by the glimpses of them I'd had in libraries. What's more, he'd succeeded despite his problems with drugs, suggesting that fiction was a forgiving industry.

I sat with my back against the cushioned headboard, scheming. Holly lay on her stomach on the sheet and drizzled a crumbly pyramid of coke onto a makeup mirror between my legs. The key, I decided, was labor. Don't withhold it. Button. Flush. Wait for green before entering the crosswalk. The revolution that Barry was predicting seemed to me impossibly far off. In the meantime, I'd place my bets on continuity. Eventually the socialists would have bragging rights, but until then the prudent seemed likely to prevail.

"He must be talented," I said to Holly, taking the mirror from her trembling hands. Someday she, too, I imagined, would go on pilgrimages, and the husband who'd finance them would be I, perhaps.

"My father doesn't produce," she said. "He *deals*."

My spirits sank. The coke went up my nose. They met in a small explosion of emotion. Disappointment crashed into euphoria, yielding a third state: delirium. I walked around for a minute to clear my thoughts.

"The dealers make the artists rich," I said, peering into the mirror world of dresses. They weren't identical, I saw. Every other one was white.

"My father's not that sort of dealer. He sells Old Masters. Italian. Flemish. Like that little Vermeer above the sofa."

"I didn't notice it. A real Vermeer?" I dug in one of my nostrils with a pinkie nail and tried to dislodge a coke crumb that was hanging there, intending to crush and reuse it.

"It's invisible where they put it. It needs rehanging. A piece can appraise for all the black in Africa, but if it's too small in the context of its space, it may as well not exist," said Holly.

"I'm thinking you should call down and get your Jaguar."

"You're bolting," said Holly. "You're sick of me. I bore you."

"I want to drive out to the ocean."

"But it's winter."

"Not to swim in it, just to walk," I said.

"How spiritual. How literary. I forget all you bookish types aren't fun like Truman."

"Truman has problems, Holly. He has ghosts."

"*Fun* ghosts."

"You don't want to go?"

"If you do. Sure."

Holly phoned for her car and fetched a coat and gloves. I wondered how she knew the weather had changed; it felt like we hadn't left the tower for days. We summoned the elevator to the living room and as we stepped into it, she said, "Truman thinks I'm named after the Holly in the book he wrote. I said I was. Sometimes I'm such a liar around old men."

"Which book?"

She stared at me. "You're kidding?"

"A book I should know?"

"If you study English, yes."

"English isn't only about books now."

"What else is it about?"

I couldn't tell her.

Down on the street, out front, the car was waiting, waxed and shining, its motor softly roaring. A doorman let Holly into the driver's seat as I walked around to my side. My door was locked. I knocked on the window. Holly didn't glance over. She settled a hand on the shift knob, engaged the gears, and glided off into a stream of uptown traffic, slowing for a red light, then surging forward and disappearing between two vans.

I dug in my pockets for money to buy a bus ticket, found some change and some crumpled dollar bills, and walked away from the cold shadow of the UN.

---

O NE NIGHT, ANOTHER BAD NIGHT—I COULDN'T SEEM TO
stop heaping them on myself—the eyes of a dead Irish poet pre-
served my soul.

I was attending a Joy Division gathering in the filthy
kitchen of a house where some architecture students lived. Suspended inside a mound of orange Jell-O were dozens of plastic
army men. They brandished bayonets and hurled grenades.
Now and then a party guest would fork a hunk of Jell-O into
his mouth and spit out a figurine onto the floor. I stepped on
one of them in my stocking feet and thought I'd been bitten by
a rat. The Jell-O was made with vodka, I learned, not water,
and laced with a substance called MDA. People poked at the
mound to make it wobble and the rest of the kitchen wobbled
with it.

"I don't understand the toy soldiers," I said to somebody.

"They're a statement on militarism."

"Opposing it?"

"Why? Do you support it?" asked the architect.

"I don't think anyone supports it."

"Aside from the majority."

"Right. Them."

Fearing exposure as a latent reactionary, I hustled upstairs and hid out in a bedroom. It was still hard for me to be against things that I'd grown up being for. Though the point of my high-school social-studies classes had seemed to be that our nation had its faults—racism, poverty, and so on—we'd been led to think that they were temporary. They'd be remedied someday by young people like us, by applying the lessons we'd learned in social studies.

I shivered as the bedroom changed shape around me. The walls and windows rotated and buckled—cubism coming true. The shrinkage of space into confining rectangles forced me to tuck my arms against my sides, press my legs together, and lie down flat. Then a new plane pushed down against my brow.

I turned my head to the side and there it was: *The Collected Poems of W. B. Yeats*. The photograph on its cover, old and silvery, showed a sorrowful, consoling face wearing a modest pair of wire-rimmed glasses. The face had an infinitely layered humanity. I wished it belonged to an ancestor. It loved me. It loved me as part of everything else it loved. The face reminded me of Uncle Admiral's, and I spoke to it out loud.

"Help get me out of this," I pleaded. "I'll do anything. Tell me what to do."

Yeats's answer was: "Try to sing, my son."

I was enrolled then in a poetry workshop taught by the editor of the anthology that had introduced me to "free verse" back in Taylors Falls. Professor Birch had the sort of curly hair that seems to indicate a curly mind. He was a few years too young to be my father and a few years too old to be my friend. For the girls he was just the right age, though. They adored him.

Birch's fondest admirer was Tessa Marchman, the trim blond daughter of two neurologists. Tessa and I were Birch's favorites, the students he called on to settle standoffs over the value of other students' poetry. Our own work couldn't have been more different. Tessa's poems focused on harrowing emotions—grief, self-loathing, panic—while mine were concerned with grander matters such as the creeping loss of "personhood" in an era of technological change. How I'd hit on this theme I wasn't sure, but the more time I spent on it the more convinced I grew that I'd borrowed it. I invented an alter ego, "Bittman," and in my poems I stretched him on the rack of mechanization and macroeconomics. In class, Tessa praised my poems as "Kafkaesque," but I could tell she didn't like them. She clearly preferred Professor Birch's work, which dealt with death and sex and feelings and left out the politics and negativity.

One day after class I walked Tessa to her room, determined to win her over to my cause. Without being pressured, she invited me up, but I found her manner impenetrable. Perhaps the invitation was mere politeness.

"Herbal tea or black?" she asked me, holding out a tray. Her room, unlike mine, was orderly and welcoming.

"Herbal tea isn't tea," I said. "It's herbs."

"Which means you want black."

"Not really. I just want tea."

"You're prickly," said Tessa.

It was true. Her crush on Birch annoyed me. The man was

a weakling, I felt, a soft romantic whose work didn't venture beyond his own five senses. But I didn't trust my senses anymore, let alone their depiction of the world. To me, an aspiring deconstructionist, the world was an orchestrated deception devised to soothe and numb. It resembled Tessa's dorm room. Stuffed animals paraded on her windowsills. Cheerful fabrics draped the chairs. The books were arranged on their shelves by height and color. And yet, at the center of all this lively neatness, lived a sad and frightened child of doctors whose poetry spoke of wounds and storms and chains. I saw right through the girl.

I let her know this over tea.

"I'm dark in my writing," she explained, "so I can look on the bright side in my real life."

"Your writing is a lie, in other words." I had no right to say this. If I'd lived according to the sentiments that dominated my Bittman poems, I wouldn't be in college but in Alaska, tucked away in a cabin with guns and canned goods. I was trying to sing, but my songs were bleak and paranoid.

"I think we both know why you're here," said Tessa. "To take me. To possess your rival." Keeping her cup and saucer on her lap, she leaned forward to make the conquest easier.

I moved ahead, but not robustly. I didn't appreciate being so swiftly fathomed. Our tea-flavored mouths barely mingled before they parted. Tessa tried to gaze into my eyes after our kiss, but I looked down. We hadn't connected. I gathered my wits and ventured another kiss. She tolerated it briefly, then left her chair and picked up a stuffed zebra.

"You're saying my work is a game. It's inauthentic."

"Come back here," I said. "I don't know what I'm saying. I don't even know why I'm saying it. Just kiss me."

"Who wants to kiss an inauthentic poet? Or sleep with one? Or see one naked?"

"Come over here. I'll show you. Please."

Tessa stayed put. She stroked her fuzzy toy. It had become a grudge match, our encounter, and the charges she'd leveled at herself had actually been aimed at me, I feared.

"I'll go," I said. "I'm sorry all this happened."

Tessa shuddered and started sobbing. Fake, I decided. Overplayed. I considered calling her bluff by wrapping my arms around her and sinking my teeth into her neck. As I dragged her toward the bed, she'd probably try to pull away or kick me, but I'd renew my assault and she'd give up. Then what? My hunch was she'd slay me with a snicker in the middle of my triumph.

"I'll see you in the workshop" was how I left it.

"Come back."

But I couldn't. Someone had to win this.


"It's the best thing I've written so far this year," I said, crossing my legs and unfolding a sheet of paper. "Of course, I'm open to comments and suggestions." Then I recited my sonnet on militarism.

"That was Bittman again?" somebody asked me. This was a common maneuver in the workshop: dismissing a poem by feigning inattention.

"It's part of a series, so I didn't name him, but, yes, it's Bittman. Or a simulacra."

"Simulacrum," said Birch, a real professor after all.

With one drop of blood, the workshop became a hunt. It opened with a few potshots, a few "reactions," but soon my classmates were firing on automatic, using the force discharged by each critique to slam new rounds into their chambers. Tessa fluttered an earlobe with an index finger, pretending to be above the fray. Birch adopted the same attitude. It was hard for me not to view them as conspirators. Or were they lovers? It wouldn't be unprecedented. Another poetry teacher, a pal of Birch's, had been run off the campus a couple of months earlier after seducing an unknown number of students, one of whom had squealed to Nassau Hall.

"To me, your main trouble, Walter," someone said, "is Bittman's supposed nemesis. He's up against *something*—the government? the system?—but you never tell us who or what. And it's not an equal fight. The world just rolls over him. He's *passive*."

"Overpowered," I said, "isn't passive. I hear you, though. Maybe if I sharpened up my verbs—"

"Or gave him a personality," said someone.

"Or any traits at all," said someone else.

"My gripe against Bittman," announced a third voice, "is that he seems incapable of love."

"He also refuses to take responsibility."

"He's a cipher."

"A device."

I held up a hand. "Can I handle those in order?"

Chuckles broke out. The abandonment felt absolute when I looked at Birch for help and caught him with his eyes shut, leaning back, absently clicking the button on a ballpoint protruding from a front pocket of his jeans. In a poetry workshop, conspicuous detachment didn't mean neutrality, I'd learned, but agreement with the prevailing line of criticism.

"I think we've been unfair," said Tessa. "Walter had it right. He had a point. Bittman's not passive at all. He's overwhelmed."

I tightened my stomach, waiting for the jab.

"And *of course* he knows how to love. It's in the *form*."

"Explain," someone said. I was curious myself.

"The *sonnet* form. Sonnets are love songs," Tessa said. "I'm surprised no one got that."

"I am, too," said Birch, leading me to think he hadn't slept with her but was still in the process of wooing her. Why else support her in this silliness?

Afterward, over pizza in the student center, I asked Tessa why she'd been so charitable. She credited her "good Midwestern upbringing." I'd had one of these upbringings myself, but it was gone, it seemed. If it had been Tessa's poem the class was slaughtering, I knew I wouldn't have intervened. Out of shame for this hypothetical failure and hoping to break through to intimacy, I confessed that my poems were all a sham and that Bittman was a hybrid version of Eliot's Prufrock and Berryman's Henry, two famously beleaguered characters from the Norton anthologies. Then I humbled myself further by disclosing that militarism didn't bother me. Maintaining an army, a navy, and an air force was America's right, I said. Our nation had enemies.

"I want us to make love," I added. "Now."

Tessa laid a napkin on her pizza slice to sop up the red grease.

"You don't want to? I thought you wanted to," I said.

She lifted the napkin by one corner and set it beside her paper plate.

"But I just bared my soul to you. I practically admitted I'm a *Republican*."

"*Are* you?"

"Not really."

"Then why pretend to be?"

"Because I get tired of pretending I'm a communist."

"So why not just stop pretending altogether?"

I thought about this for a while. "You first," I said.

"We're just too different. Our styles. Our approaches. Plus, I suspect your motives, I'm afraid. This is all about competition, not attraction."

"Let's make it about sex, then."

"Can't be done."

"Because you're in love with Birch?"

"His sensibility."

"Well, I'm in love with Yeats's sensibility. That doesn't mean I want to go to bed with him."

Tessa sprinkled garlic on her slice and raised it to her tidy mouth. I folded my empty plate in half and headed off to dump it in a trash can. Literature had torn Tessa and me apart, or prevented us from merging in the first place. That was its role in the world, I'd started to fear: to conjure up disagreements that didn't matter and inspire people to act on them as though they mattered more than anything. Without literature, humans would all be one. Warfare was simply literature in arms. The pen was the reason man *invented* the sword.

Week in and week out, Birch's workshop proved me right. We sang and we fought. We fought over our songs. Finally, by the end of the semester, all we could sing about were our scars, our wounds.

# Eleven

Nantucket, the Island, the Cape, the Vineyard—I couldn't distinguish among the seaside getaways where so many of my classmates said they intended to spend the summer vacation. When they spoke of visiting these spots, they used the preposition "on," as in "I'll be *on* the Cape for August." When referring to Minnesota, I used "in," which didn't sound as good, I thought. But there was no other way to say it.

Then, in late May, my father called with news. While on a business trip in Munich, Germany, he'd landed me a summer job, he said, working at what he described over the phone as an "internationally famous nightspot" where "various Hemingway types" hung out. He said he'd been drinking in the place one night and struck up a conversation with its owner, Herr Blick, an American expatriate, about my ambitions as a writer. Herr Blick, whom my father lauded as "a true gentleman," had agreed right away to fly me over and pay me to help out behind the bar. I told my father I'd do it. Though I'd learned through the years to fear the consequences of his impulsive decisions ("We'll farm these fields with horses!"), I feared going home even more. They might not like me there.

Herr Blick met me at the Munich airport. The first impression he made was that of a master at making first impressions. His handshake had a practiced-feeling sincerity and was augmented by a hearty shoulder squeeze that lasted awhile and almost became a rub. His muscular body seemed younger and better maintained than his square and sunburned fortyish face. He insisted on carrying both of my duffel bags for me, hoisting them off the luggage carousel with what looked like a weight-lifter's concern for minimizing back strain.

Instead of dropping me at the fraternity house where one of my father's German lawyer colleagues had arranged to rent a room for me, Herr Blick parked his sporty Mercedes near his bar and gave me a walking tour of central Munich. The two historical figures he kept citing as he pointed out various ornate buildings were Adolf Hitler and Mad King Ludwig. Hitler, he told me, had gotten his public start here, and Ludwig had kept his harem here. Herr Blick passed lightly over this detail, not mentioning that the harem consisted of boys.

The fraternity building was near the bar, wedged into the middle of a block. It appeared to be vacant for the season. On my way up the narrow staircase to my room I passed an alcove sheltering a pedestal bearing a marble bust of Julius Caesar. The art in the hallways featured shields and eagles and down one dim corridor I caught a glimpse of a spacious torture chamber. On hooks on the walls above a bare wood floor hung a macabre array of masks and weapons. I tiptoed closer: fencing gear.

My room was a cell, austere and cramped. I vowed to stay

out of it except to sleep. I doubted I'd get much sleep, however. According to Herr Blick, my shifts at the bar would run from seven at night until three in the morning, six nights a week. I contemplated this schedule and my surroundings and determined that learning German that summer would not be among my primary ambitions. I set myself a more vital task: survival. That, and reading the only book I'd brought: Malcolm Lowry's *Under the Volcano*, a novel about the final day on earth of a drunken, lovelorn British diplomat living in Mexico during World War II. I'd opened it somewhere over the Atlantic, been seized by its tone of clotted doom, and pushed ahead through its dense, allusive paragraphs, hoping that the myths and masterworks floating out of my reach behind its pages would somehow drift into my reach if I persisted. From the preface, I'd learned that the novel drew on Dante, Homer, Shakespeare, and other immortals, which raised the tantalizing prospect of obtaining sweeping erudition by reading a single book.

My job at the bar required no German, luckily. It demanded almost no speech at all. My immediate boss—to whom I handed clean glasses that had been briefly dunked in soapy water and partially dried with a thin towel—was a local celebrity named Wilhelm who specialized in multilayered cocktails of luminous coloration. Against the unspotted whiteness of his starched jacket, his crinkly gray hair and sinewy, tanned face were savagely vivid and alluring. I was in awe of him, as were the customers. After a couple of weeks of watching him carrying on behind the bar like a six-armed pagan god, producing lighted matches from unseen pockets, juggling tumblers in the air, and sailing coasters into distant trash cans, I no longer saw the point of going back to college in the fall. This was true fame

I was witnessing, true mastery. I should stay and learn from it. Even Herr Blick deferred to Wilhelm, terrified, surely, of losing his bar's chief draw.

After counting the cash and bundling the receipts, I turned out the lights and locked the building's front door. Outside, on the street, strange men accosted me, asking "Where now?" or "What next?" in muttered German that even I could translate. I learned to brush past them with my head down. Sealed in a jar and wrapped in a brown bag was my nightly ration of stolen schnapps, which I drank deeply from once I'd run the gauntlet, as a toast to myself for reaching safety. By the time I passed Caesar's head on the dark stairway, I was feeling tight and tipsy. Then I lay down with *Under the Volcano* and finished off the jar. The book had begun to seriously haunt me. Its references to Dante still eluded me, but I empathized with its crumbling protagonist.

One night Herr Blick dispatched me to the kitchen to make croque monsieurs and espressos for his tablemates. The little spouts on the coffee machine clogged up. To clear them, I had to kneel down on the floor and poke at their openings with a twisted dishrag. I felt a presence behind me as I worked. Then I heard a belt unbuckling. I didn't move. I didn't turn around. I prayed that the presence, which wore Herr Blick's cologne, would reconsider its intentions.

"Hot weather makes me horny."

I held position, facing the machine. "I'm not a homosexual," I said.

"Horny's horny. Who said it was gay? Is that what you Princeton boys think? That horny's gay?"

"I'm sorry, Herr Blick. That isn't what I meant."

"You got that from your perverted prep school, probably."

"I didn't go to prep school."

"Then why the attitude?"

"I didn't realize it was attitude."

"To me—to an army brat—it's attitude."

I heard a zipper I hadn't known was down being zipped back up. The presence retreated. Ten minutes later, pretending nothing had happened, I delivered the food and coffee to Herr Blick's table, fussing over the placement of plates and silverware. A German girl at the table, early twenties, ample chest, high cheekbones, reddish hair, appraised me as I stumbled through my duties. Later, when I was back behind the bar, she came up and introduced herself as Hannah, but I assumed she was addressing Wilhelm, who was pouring a whip of shining Blue Curaçao into a silver cocktail shaker.

"This is my number," Hannah said in English, pushing a paper napkin toward me. "Ring me on Saturday. We'll discuss Herr Blick. I'll show you my squat and we can see a play that's being performed by my collective. Do you admire the work of Dario Fo?"

It was Europe. Why not be honest? "I don't know him."

"Super," said Hannah. "Soon you'll know him well."

But my father made other plans for me that Saturday. He accepted an invitation on my behalf from Dr. Frisch, the German attorney who'd gotten me my tiny room. The invitation, which I couldn't decline, was to a festival way out in the countryside. It celebrated the wedding anniversary of a medieval Bavarian princess.

Dr. Frisch picked me up at seven in the morning and drove

at high speeds in his sedan deep into what he termed "the land itself."

"How are you liking it at the Corps?" he asked me. He meant the sinister fraternity, and the pride in his voice suggested he'd once belonged to it. So did the fencing scar on one of his cheeks. "Have you conversed yet with any of the brothers?"

I explained that my schedule prevented any such contacts. The young men conducted their sword fights in the mornings and were gone by the time that I woke up. "That is a shame," Dr. Frisch said. He seemed angry. "I warned your father that your job would isolate you from the true German society. To labor on a good dairy would be much preferable."

The route into the village hosting the festival was barricaded from motor traffic. We parked in a mucky field and walked to town. Dr. Frisch had the strongest walk I'd ever witnessed. His heels chopped into the sod and flung chunks back at me. While I tried to keep pace, he vented his contempt for the decadent Munich nightclub scene, asserting that it was filled with prostitutes and political subversives. "This is the wrong introduction. Corrupt. Absurd. Today will prove an antidote, I hope."

We entered a throng of costumed revelers who may or may not have had roles in the parade. Some of the ladies had flowers in their hair and some of the men carried daggers on their belts. The warm, midday air felt thick with ancient kinship. I'd discovered during my time in Germany that I had a high tolerance for foreignness, thanks, perhaps, to my first year at Princeton, but here, among the damsels and the knights, as the buglers and string players tuned their instruments and little girls dressed as fairies went dancing by, I suddenly felt so smothered by the exotic that my esophagus closed up and bouncing black dots appeared before my eyes. The problem wasn't the pageantry itself, which wasn't so different from American pageantry—also based on hats and horns—but the solemn comportment of the spectators. In the States, we grinned at dress-up holidays, but here the crowd was sober, worshipful.

We watched the procession from a balcony. A waiter circulated with a tray laden with rolled-up cold cuts and cubes of sausage. I was among some wealthy people, I sensed, but I couldn't gauge how educated they were. They licked their fingers when they ate. They drank from beer glasses with napkins stuck to them. The clues about class that I'd picked up at Princeton were useless to me here.

Beneath the terrace, ranks of heavy horses trudged through drifts of manure and flower petals, drawing old carriages filled with storybook characters. I gathered from Dr. Frisch's shifting responses—outbursts of clapping, pauses for meditation, gleams of high amusement—that the profusion of huntsmen, ladies-in-waiting, falconers, peasants, and royalty spoke to his soul in distinctive, varied ways.

"Hers is a beauty uniquely German," he said. He was waving at someone.

"Whose?" I'd looked away.

"The princess's. Our dear princess," he said. He pointed out a gilded, antique conveyance that had already passed before the balcony, its wheels cutting parallel ruts in the manure. It dawned on me then that I'd missed the main event, the glorious, folkloric climax of the day. And Dr. Frisch had noticed. His brow grew stormy.

I needed an excuse. Immediately. I'd insulted my host in a country where such things mattered.

"I'm sorry. I was lost in thought," I said.

Dr. Frisch cocked a huge German eyebrow.

"It's Herr Blick."

I described my entrapment at the coffee machine, playing to Dr. Frisch's fiercest prejudices about the degenerate climate at the bar. His bologna-colored skin went crimson. The man didn't like me much, intuition told me, but he respected me as a high-caste guest, and hearing that I'd been dishonored in his realm made icicle points of his blue eyes.

"Do nothing. I will do everything," he vowed.

While waiting for the storm to break, I spent as much time as I could with Hannah, the anarchist, in her surprisingly well-furnished squat. One day we bathed together in her tub. I asked her why the hot water was still turned on if no one was paying for it. She acted perplexed. I concluded that withholding rent was normal behavior with Hannah's generation and didn't merit any particular punishment.

As we dried off, she produced two small foil packets that she said contained a strong narcotic in fast-acting suppository form. I braced my hands on a wall as she inserted one between my parted legs. Then I returned the favor. Then we had sex. I enjoyed the directness of it all and thought once again about not returning to Princeton.

That evening we saw the Dario Fo play. The performers were Hannah's age, all unemployed, all living as she did, apparently. On nothing. The lines were in German but I could follow the story. It concerned the interrogation of a man by a group of crazy secret police. I knew from the style of the poster that the play was supposed to be a comedy, but the audience in the smoky coffeehouse showed little mirth as it unfolded. When the suspect was murdered, they finally laughed. It felt to me like revolution loomed here, but not in the fanciful way it did at Princeton. Munich's youth were preparing for a true fight. They'd do it with painkillers in their rushing bloodstreams, and if I stayed they might make me join their ranks.

"You know that the girl's a prostitute," Herr Blick said when he learned that I'd been seeing Hannah. We were upstairs in the private VIP bar, where he was throwing a party for two Englishmen who were dancing back-to-back to disco music after stripping off their shirts. My job was to top up the drinks and empty the ashtrays. Dr. Frisch hadn't come to save me yet. Where was he?

He must have heard my silent call. The next afternoon, in my room at the fraternity, he described his plan of battle, pacing the creaky floorboards in stiff black shoes. He brandished a pencil and a notepad on which he'd tabulated what I was due as a gentleman who'd been wronged in his Bavaria.

"You contracted for another five weeks of labor. Your unpaid salary will be our base. Then we will multiply it by the injury. Not only the injury to you. I feel that a factor of five is justified, but he will agree to a factor of eight or nine. If not I will speak to Wilhelm as a German and Wilhelm will do what is honorable, I know, and threaten resignation. This will work."

The speech made me want to back out of the scheme. I felt Dr. Frisch had vastly overestimated the value of my good opinion of his homeland. But I knew why he had. It was Princeton.

Princeton awed him. Its role at the forefront of theoretical physics—the subject he'd trained in before becoming a patent lawyer—was the source of his awe. We'd talked about this once.

"The factor is too high," I said. "I'll settle for the five weeks pay."

"But I will not," Dr. Frisch said. "Now we go."

We surprised Herr Blick in his office above the barroom. He was counting his money from the night before and tapping one foot to a perky Euro-pop song playing on his desktop radio. When he saw us, he tried to stash the cash in a drawer that was open on his right, but Dr. Frisch stopped him with a word of German. He then brought forth his notepad, tore a page off, and placed it on the blotter on Herr Blick's desk. There were no negotiations. The bills that made up the fine were counted twice—once by each party, the sinner and the avenger—before being placed in the pit of my right hand.

"Now Walter Kirn is whole," said Dr. Frisch.

I felt a bit guilty, but he was right. For it was then, that day, in Munich, Germany, as I filled my pockets with blackmail money extracted for a slight against my dignity (and again that night, with Hannah, when I bought beer for a table full of anarchists who thanked me with a noisy, sloshing toast), that I at last knew my power and my status as what I'd forgotten I was: a Princeton man.

I was ready to go back.

# Twelve

M**Y CLASSMATES' LOOKS HAD CHANGED OVER THE SUM-**
mer. Some of them now resembled adults. It had nothing to do
with the loss of baby fat. It had nothing to do with wisdom in
their eyes. It was their haircuts, literally their haircuts. By exper-
imentation or inspiration or simply by yielding to the wills of
experts, they'd finally found the haircuts which best suited them
and allowed them to squarely meet the world.

Not that there was just one world to meet. By my second
year at Princeton I'd catalogued a half-dozen social groups
whose members I found recognizable at middle distances of
thirty feet or so, across a quad or down a hallway, and each
of which stirred in me, for different reasons, potent feelings of
envy and contempt, longing and revulsion. All of these factions,
it seemed to me, had certain attributes I lacked and lacked certain attributes I had. And though I knew it was too late for me
to belong to any of these groups—not wholly, not permanently,
not plausibly—I hoped that by picking and choosing among
their traits I could assemble a persona that would let me belong
to me. Reason told me this project was impossible, since any "I"

fabricated from a "they" would forever regard itself, deep down, as nothing but an "it" and end up feeling lonely in its own company. But reason was not my reigning faculty then. Nor could it be, I felt, in a post-deconstructionist era of wild guesses. No, what ruled me was restlessness, disquiet, a nagging sense of missing out on things that others, more classifiable, had access to.

These others were as follows.

### Those Who'd Been on Sailboats

The tender, sheltered skin that forms the eyelids seemed to cover their entire bodies. Their enemy was sunlight, which turned their skin a pre-carcinoma scarlet, while their friend was the double gin and tonic, which flushed vitality into their capillaries. Most of them suffered from thinning hair, the males and females both, which might have explained their fondness for stupid hats. They favored straw hats when cheering the rowing crew, Princeton or prep-school team caps when jogging, canvas hats while lying in the grass, and any old hat when they were drunk, a state that was hard to diagnose in them because they held their liquor well. Sometimes they started nipping away at breakfast, if their responsibilities were light that day.

Their responsibilities seemed light on most days. Their money arrived by stealth, in neutral envelopes sent by lawyers, accountants, and trustees, though sometimes it was delayed by court proceedings in Newport or Kennebunkport or Southampton, where their semiretired parents' sloops were docked. The names of these craft remembered beloved ancestors (*Aunt Melissa*), alluded to family commercial interests (*Bid and*

*Call*), or displayed an inbred nautical wit (*Triton's Trifle*). I saw a few of them once in coastal Connecticut, where I'd gone to the beach to pick up young foreign au pairs with a friend who'd grown up in the area. There were a lot of these girls, but they ignored us, maybe because I was swimming in cutoff jeans.

The effortlessness of the sailboat caste was their most appealing quality. If they dropped something—a pen, a book, a dollar—they scooped it back up like a ball at Wimbledon. They napped during lectures, but rarely to their detriment because they could always charm some awestruck stranger—a plump girl with a limp, a science major with untied shoelaces—into giving them copies of their notes. They danced at a pleasant low intensity, avoiding any new or tricky moves that might jostle the drinks in their right hands or stress their knees, the weakest part of them. If, toward the end of a weekend party night, you spied one puking behind a hedge, he'd grin and salute you, then carry on heaving. Later you'd see him on the dance floor joking away with some girl you'd never speak to because you didn't understand lacrosse, and lacrosse was all she had to talk about. That, and the time her madcap cousin at Andover, a guy named Topper or maybe Tuffy, released a muskrat in the records office.

For the boaters, Princeton was a lark before the real work of life began: building client lists, hiring tax advisers, courting the daughters of their fathers' partners, guiding the restoration of summer homes. This lent their time at Princeton a touch of pathos. Custom decreed that they live like there was no tomorrow, but tomorrow was coming, laden with obligations. Tradition and duty owned these kids.

Still, for about a week, I tried to ape them. I found a wall that abutted an empty courtyard and went there at night with a junk-store tennis racket to serve and rally unobserved. I'd had a few lessons in eighth-grade gym class, but I lost all of my balls by the fourth session because my strokes were too hard for the small space. I watched them ricochet off into the darkness like little yellow comets. Next I scrounged up some money to buy deck shoes. The problem was that such shoes had no charisma until they were scuffed and wrinkled and worn out. I tried to distress them by soaking them in water and tumbling them in a coin dryer. This shrunk and dehydrated the leather, causing me to get blisters when I wore them.

### Those Who Strove to Serve Mankind

They studied at the Woodrow Wilson School of Public and International Policy, a selective college within a college housed in a sprawling, stylized Greek temple barricaded from the outside world by an array of slim white columns shaped like vertical drips of Elmer's glue. The edifice, whose design was so replete with futuristic optimism that it already seemed comically defunct, faced a plaza with a broad reflecting pool whose centerpiece was an abstract sculpture evocative of the maggot-scoured remains of a giant chicken carcass. Set across the street from the main campus, the complex had no aesthetic connection to the rest of the university, which accorded with the insular nature of its pre-senatorial occupants. So crisp and determined they seemed, so sure and steady, so confident that their country would make them boss one day. Did they have doubts? Being young, they probably did, but they also had procedures for removing them, pie graph by pie graph, seminar by seminar. Someday these kids would be nothing but firm handshakes.

When they stood on the granite steps below the columns or sat on the plaza eating lunch (the largest expanse of treeless space at Princeton other than the football field), they didn't look to me like human beings but like stick figures in an architect's scale model.

What I wanted from them—the only thing I wanted; I certainly didn't want their workloads—was their seriousness, their certainty, their seeming immunity to second thoughts. The world for them was not some tricky text but a color-coded manila folder. Open it, remove the stacked white pages, scan the outline on page one, read for half an hour, walk down the hall, nod to the guards, and brief the president. The war should begin no later than next April. These short-term interest rates are unsustainable. Only three breeding pairs of black-beaked hawks remain, all of them near the Utah air force base where we're conducting Operation Parabola. "Thank you." "You're welcome, sir." "How's the family?" "Excellent." "Run today?" "Fifteen kilometers." "Good man."

A little faith in the establishment and in the orderly cosmos for which it stood wouldn't hurt me, I decided. With it, I might be able to decline the next hit of mescaline from Adam and pass the sand ashtray outside of Firestone Memorial Library without digging for a butt. From orthodoxy might come self-esteem, even a measure of discipline, perhaps.

I started hanging around the Woodrow Wilson School ("Woody Woo," the students called it) in the hope of absorbing its can-do spirit. I poked my nose into the lecture halls, which took the form of austere amphitheaters where one might imagine illustrious alumni such as Paul Volcker and John Foster Dulles sketching diagrams on the wide blackboards. Unlike Yale and Harvard, Princeton didn't breed leaders, historically, but loyal lieutenants, trusted aides, self-effacing senior bureaucrats.

One afternoon on the plaza, eating yogurt, I got to chatting with a girl who hoped to help institute universal health care. It would be free to everyone, she said. She seemed to be talking about me.

"What are you doing later?"

"Studying."

"After you're done studying," I said.

"Sleeping, probably. If I can sleep. I haven't been able to lately. It's terrible."

"What keeps you up at night?" I couldn't imagine.

"Worrying that I should be studying, not sleeping."

My chance encounters at Woody Woo were like that. They apprised me of concerns I'd never thought about. Some were profound concerns. Epidemics. Border wars. Land distribution in Central and South America. I grew ashamed of my solipsism, my foolishness. The sun on the naked plaza seemed to spotlight them, eventually driving me back into the shade.

### Those Who Never Raised Their Eyes

They were scientists, mathematicians, and engineers. Life was a distraction to them. They ate and drank to sustain their neural chemistries, but only while doing more constructive things such as walking to the lab or punching calculators. Somehow, someday, they'd reproduce, but that phase was not yet upon them, blessedly. For now they were free to decline communication and dress in pants that didn't reach their shoes. They were free to read while climbing stairs and free not to say they were sorry when they bumped into people. People didn't expect them to apologize. People didn't see them as other people.

I coveted their oblivious self-sufficiency, but I coveted their silence most. I was tired of having to blabber to survive. Sometimes I pretended to be one of them. I'd cross the campus staring at the sidewalk, projecting patterns onto the cement. I'd baffle my friends by declining to say hi to them. I'd ride the elevator three floors down into the deepest strata of the library and systematically pace the aisles between the acres of tall shelves. I'd go to bed without undressing and clip a light to a book and turn the pages with tick-tock regularity, paying the same attention to difficult passages as I did to patches of dialogue. I made notes with colored pencils: black, red, green. Black meant this part is worthy of memorization. Red meant this part might be flawed or dubious. Green meant this part called for fuller analysis, should I ever find the time. I read James Joyce's *Portrait of the Artist as a Young Man* by precisely this method, my pencils hovering. The girl who'd later lose her will to live by mistaking herself for Anna Karenina and Adam for Vronsky spied me at this work when she came to retrieve a book she'd loaned me.

"How can you hear Joyce's music if you keep stabbing it with pencils?"

"I can't afford to read for music anymore. I'm reading to put this behind me and move on."

But English could not be reduced to engineering. When I put down a book that I'd marked up, it left my mind so thoroughly that when I picked it up again, the characters were aliens, the story unfamiliar, and the setting no place I'd ever visited. I was toiling twice as hard for one-eighth or one-sixteenth of the gains. And my few friendships were dissolving.

It was Adam who snapped me out of it. He aced an exam, without doing any work, on which I got a B after nights of study. I'd forgotten to dapple my answers with theory words. I'd forgotten to use "gestural."

"Plus, I was stoned," Adam told me when the grades arrived. "What the hell did you think you were doing?"

"Remaining focused."

"Play to your strengths," he said.

"They feel like weaknesses."

"Not if you play them for all they're worth," he said.

### Those Who Pursued Disintegration Fully

They were injecting cocaine when I came in. They pricked their arms, drew the blood up through the needle, let the blood swirl in the fluid in the barrel, and then pressed the plunger while tipping back their heads. Barry was there, but the other kids in the circle were strangers to me. They didn't look like students. One of them had ball bearings instead of eyes. Another one had cheeks like sneaker soles, with repeating V shapes stamped into them. I found out why. Before I'd wandered in, the guy had been passed out on a rug woven with the same pattern. They'd revived him by dripping the coke solution on his tongue. Now he was revving. He flicked the fine-gauge needle, clearing it of bubbles, then jabbed himself in the soft crook of his elbow. "Damn right!" he yelled. Then he ran out of the room.

"Your turn," said Barry.

"It isn't sterile."

"I'm holding it over a candle. You're watching me do it."

"My mother's a nurse. That doesn't work."

I stayed to help in case someone overdosed. AIDS wasn't yet a fear, just heart attacks. Barry appeared to have one after he stuck himself, but only a mild one, a tremor. After a lapse into pallor and clamminess, he stuttered back to life. Then we went off on a tear of Marxist rhetoric that only ended when ball-bearing eyes clamped a veiny hand over his mouth. By then, the rest of the users had the jitters. One was facing a wall and running in place. One was bickering with the ghoul beside him about a girl they'd both seduced—together, apparently, on the same night—who was complaining of having caught a bug that the first guy believed came from the ghoul and the ghoul was blaming on a third guy. But they all had it now, this bug, or feared they did. I strained to hear the girl's name. They talked too fast, though. Then, suddenly, they were talking about music—bands they'd seen and records they'd bought, musicians they'd personally spent time around. I discerned from this that they all came from New York and had known one another, through school, for years and years. Other than that, the only resemblance that I detected among them was a distracted indifference to one another. When the drugs were gone, so were their bonds. Some wind arose that they offered no resistance to and blew them from the room.

I would have to be myself.

# Thirteen

My closest friend as a junior was V., a Pakistani boy who'd disappointed his family—and even, as he told it, his nation's leaders—by leaving his intended major, electrical engineering, for philosophy. He claimed that his decision was purely intellectual, but I suspected a social motive. Among the campus's tastemaking elite, philosophy was in vogue just then, especially the arcane linguistic variety that allowed one to brandish Ludwig Wittgenstein's *Tractatus Logico-Philosophicus*, whereas engineering was deemed unsuitable for anyone other than indentured third worlders whose governments were paying their tuition in return for future work designing missiles and irrigation projects.

This had been V.'s deal. Once he broke it, whether out of conviction or in deference to fashion, he couldn't go home again. That made two of us.

I met V. on one of my rare visits to the labyrinth of open stacks housed in the bombproof trio of subbasements beneath the Firestone Library. The place was designed like an iceberg, with most of its square footage buried and a fortresslike outcropping on top. Standing on the plaza near its entrance, light-ing yet another cigarette as a way of postponing going inside, I could imagine a legion of the literate aiming crossbows from the parapets at onrushing armies of hollering barbarians. The con-frontation might end in countless casualties, but the books would survive, civilization would endure. Not me, though—I'd probably be slaughtered. Firestone intimidated me, breeding a sort of cultural vertigo whenever I found myself in its vaulted lobby presenting my puny ID card to the guards. When the bat-tle for civilization finally came I'd probably be stranded outside its walls.

I went there that evening not to read but to listen to tapes of illustrious dead poets reciting their best-known works. The tapes were a bit of labor-saving luck that I'd heard about from an older English major who was even lazier than I was. You weren't allowed to enjoy them in your room, though; you had to consume them in the library, through pairs of gigantic cush-ioned headphones that might have been surplus from NASA Mission Control. I chose Sylvia Plath and Robert Lowell that night because I was in the mood for doomed New Englanders. Plath's voice, pressured and brutal, frightened me because I could truly imagine her alive, which helped me picture her killing herself, too, while Lowell's voice was so antique and magisterial that I couldn't believe he'd ever lived on earth. Af-ter hanging the headphones on their hook and signaling the at-tendant that I was finished, I decided to ride the elevator downstairs and look for a volume of Lowell's poetry with an au-thor photo on the jacket. I wanted assurance of his materiality.

About an hour later, while waiting in the checkout line to present my dubious credentials as a trustworthy borrower of masterpieces, I fell into a conversation with V., whom I found instantly engaging. He was the first brown person I'd ever spoken to on an approximately equal basis, and I liked the slim symmetries of his face and figure. I also liked the way he dressed. His dark V-necked sweater, though slightly pilled and stretched into shapelessness at the cuffs and hem, seemed effortlessly collegiate. His black shoes were stout and nicely scuffed. His pants were proper pants, not jeans. He dressed as I fancied the young Lowell had dressed, and as I wished I dressed, with offhand British elegance.

Immanuel Kant was the topic that broke the ice for us. My knowledge of the impeccable old German came from a philosophy class whose internationally respected professor taught that Kant, with his clockwork daily strolls and monastic temperament, was the last in a line of ambitious eminences who'd sought to "ground" ethics, morals, and metaphysics in a realm of changeless "authenticity." Kant had almost succeeded in this feat, but the fact that he hadn't proved, said the professor, that the whole endeavor was futile and ought to be abandoned for the pursuit of a humbler form of wisdom: "the conversation." This was fine with me. Never did I consider it bad news when someone who'd devoted decades to mastering a knotty subject reported that the subject, in the end, wasn't worth devoting decades to.

Our chat about Kant saw V. and me across the Firestone plaza to Nassau Street and down the staircase of the Annex. We found a table near a wall, close enough to the crowd to feel its warmth but far away enough to hear each other speak. I felt invigorated in V.'s company. Whatever the schools were like in Pakistan, they clearly did a better job than ours in instilling analytic agility and at least the beginnings of erudition. Given no more than a phrase ("the conversation," say), V. could cite a set of classical precepts that were both plausible and graspable, good for hours of heightened interaction. I felt, in his company as in no one else's, that my bullshitting was a defensible activity, a circular approach to real enlightenment. And I felt flattered when he listened to me. Here was a young man who represented the best of the best of an entire country—of an entire *people*, as I saw it—and I was holding his attention.

Drugs played no part in our relationship. Ours were purely sober colloquies, fueled by aspiration and affection. We walked through the leaves, past sunlit spires of stone, attacking the roots of language and understanding with hatchets of iron skepticism. Reality softened around us. We came to regard ourselves as lonely Nietzscheans who'd cast off thick veils of prejudicial nonsense and emerged as unencumbered wills. "I'm leaning over. I'm picking up this rock. I could throw it," I said, "and break that window, but instead I'll hold on to it. Because I'm free."

Later that fall we sat by a canal and watched the crew team row past in its trim vessels. By then we'd declared ourselves "phenomenologists." I wasn't sure what this required of us besides a refusal to meet the gazes of students who were still mired in what we termed, dismissively, as "consensual certitude."

"After you graduate," I said, "how long will they let you stay in the U.S.?"

"Indefinitely, I hope. Provided, of course, that I find secure employment or continue with my studies."

I nodded, chilled. I'd given not a single thought, I realized, to the question of what I might do once I left Princeton.

"I'd like to teach someday," V. said. He reached for an

acorn, pried its cap off, and tossed it into the canal—another one of our little shows of freedom.

"What subject?" I asked him. "Philosophy?"

"Perhaps. Though I'm not convinced it can be taught. Philosophy may be over. You?" he said.

"Maybe poetry."

"Teach it?"

"No, just write it."

"For whom? For what sort of audience?"

This stumped me. I sat on the grass and watched the boats slide past.

"I'm sorry," said V.

"It's fine." I fingered an oak twig.

"All poets have the same audience. The Silence."

One keen winter night we set out down Prospect Avenue with the intention of crashing a party at one of the eating clubs that wouldn't have us. The spring before, in a process known as "bicker," the five remaining selective clubs—Ivy, Cottage, Tiger, Colonial, and Cap and Gown—had interviewed and chosen new members. This ritual had occurred without my knowledge. I only found out about bicker afterward, when I glimpsed a Joy Division friend of mine crossing a quad one afternoon with a pair of hearty-looking new pals. I made inquiries. I learned that my friend now belonged to the Tiger Club, the ale-drenched, reactionary redoubt of Princeton's most stalwart young misogynists. Not only was the all-male Tiger fighting a headline-making lawsuit against a rejected aspirant named Sally, but a number of its members had been implicated in the unwitting videotaping of a drunken female guest during a sex act that might have been coerced. That someone I knew had sought favor with such brutes shocked and astonished me at first, but I couldn't blame him once I'd thought about it. They'd made him feel wanted, apparently.

V. seemed serene about having been shut out by the campus's high-society gatekeepers. He took his meals in a campus dining hall with a trio of other students from the subcontinent, as he'd taught me to call his geographic homeland, while I'd joined the bitterly nonconformist Terrace Club, home to Princeton's proudest rejects. Though the nearly bankrupt Terrace took all comers, we (the wounded seventeen of us who ate beneath its leaking roof and danced on its warped linoleum floors) considered it exclusive anyway. We construed the fact that the place conferred no status to mean that status didn't concern us, which made us rare individuals indeed. I subsidized my membership by working part-time in the club's anarchic kitchen, helping concoct inexpensive meatless meals at the direction of the stoned head chef, most of whose dishes were inspired by recipes in the *Moosewood Cookbook*, a best-selling guide to taste-free dining. Assisting me in the task of blending hummus and garnishing it with sprouts was Edmond, a neo-pagan extrovert who liked to strip naked when the room got hot, exposing the food to casual contamination by his freely streaming armpit sweat and abundant body hair. Far from regarding this practice as unsanitary, Edmond believed it to be nourishing, since food, as he told me many times, ought to absorb the spirits of its preparers.

On the way to the party V. and I talked Wittgenstein, loudly, so others could hear us in the dark. "*Whereof one cannot speak, thereof one must be silent*." We also debated "the purpose of love." V. held that love had no purpose—love just *was*—while I asserted that its purpose was to induce in the lover a condition of "dual-beholding," whatever that might be. Girls went by as we spoke, but not a lot of them, and few who were available to our kind. Just twelve years after Princeton had gone coed, the campus gender ratio still favored males by a considerable margin, placing a premium on pretty women that only rich boys and quarterbacks could pay. Our shape-shifting, agile, approval-seeking brains may have entitled us to live and study with the children of the ruling class, but not to mate with them.

This was the system's great flaw, and it enraged us. A pure meritocracy, we'd discovered, can only promote; it can't legitimize. It can confer success but can't grant knighthood. For that it needs a class beyond itself: the high-born genealogical peerage that aptitude testing was created to overthrow.

So far, the experiment hadn't worked.

Somehow we slipped past the door into a room jammed with handsome, arrhythmic dancers wearing a unisex wardrobe of khaki trousers and pastel polo shirts with turned-up collars. A few of them danced as couples, shouting at each other over the music and tossing their heads back in showy gaiety, but most of them aimed their movements at the whole group. When V. and I tried to join the fun, the crowd contracted and squeezed us out in a kind of collective immune response. V. wandered off somewhere, but I persevered, managing finally to find a gap in the jiggling collective. After being battered by the broad chest of a red-faced, hostile-looking athlete with a much-autographed cast on his right arm, I retreated to a smaller hole. I fixed a lunatic smile on my face and bopped to the beat in perfect isolation, thinking that if I kept the act up long enough someone would let me be her partner.

It didn't happen. All female backs stayed turned. I slunk off to the professionally staffed bar, and in no time I was drunk and plotting revenge.

I targeted a girl with pearl earrings whose solid, columnar figure, husky voice, and rubber-banded sheaf of wheaty hair held no physical attraction for me but aroused my inner revolutionary. Like a frustrated stableboy in an old novel, I wanted to seduce and ruin her. Amazingly, we ended up alone on the floor of an empty upstairs room. The girl lay under me in a white bra heavily armored with wires and foam padding. She kissed me with an aggressive suction that actually drew blood from my chapped lips. She tugged at my zipper and uttered bold obscenities. Her passion was frank, elemental, and overwhelming, permitting me no illusion of domination. I was servicing a fair-haired warrior goddess, bred to lead and to give birth to leaders.

But she was drunker than I knew; as the act began in earnest, she fell asleep—a total power outage. Should I press on? Here was a chance to vent a primal fury on a symbol of everything that tortured me.

I couldn't do it. I fled downstairs, found V., and made him leave with me. On the walk back to his room he said, "What assholes."

"We're just as bad," I said. I didn't explain.

We sobered up in V.'s room by drinking coffee. As he tended to when pressured by strong emotion, he launched into one of his disquisitions on language, and I chimed in with my own thoughts now and then, though my mind was on the girl back at the club. V.'s point, I gathered, was his usual one: words referred to other words, not to the world, and the finest, grandest words, such as "nature" and "God," referred to nothing. Or maybe I misunderstood. It hardly mattered. It had been years since I'd known what I was talking about, and I no longer expected such conversations to be conclusive or enlightening. They were catechisms, incantations. They reminded me of a short-lived high-school class in which we'd tried to learn German phonetically by repeating sentences from tapes.

Tonight, though, I couldn't bear the posing, and I understood why V.'s government was mad at him: he might have built great public-works projects for them, but now he was incapable of building anything. I excused myself to use the bathroom. I filled a glass of water from the tap, looked in the mirror, and beheld an absence—nothing but the reflected door behind me and a bathrobe hanging on a hook. Where was my face? I knew it still existed because I could feel it with my fingertips, but I couldn't find it with my eyes—a hallucination in reverse.

"I need a doctor," I told V. when I came back. "How late is the clinic open?"

He ignored me. He'd been holding a thought about Hegel all this time and was writing it down so that he wouldn't forget it later. I left him and walked back down Prospect Avenue, thinking that if I could find the girl I'd left there and share a normal human word with her, it would help me see my face again. But the party was over and the door was bolted.

I didn't have to wait long for my crack-up.

## Chapter Fourteen

DURING A CHAUCER LECTURE THE NEXT SEMESTER I LOST the ability to discern the boundaries between spoken words. Professor F., a venerable medievalist who was one of my favorites among the faculty because of his clarity and wit, opened his mouth and out flowed streams of nonsense with no meter, no structure, no definition. I closed my notebook, which I rarely wrote in, and managed to isolate a few short phrases from the slushy, garbled flow. But I couldn't link them into sentences. My sense of time disintegrated, too. From the moment the lecture turned to mush to the moment students left their seats, several hours seemed to pass. I couldn't believe, when I exited the building, that it was still light out.

"Allotherwalt," I heard someone say.

I scrammed.

I bought a cup of coffee at the student center, avoiding conversation with the cashier, and wandered around the campus for a while, thinking that what I needed was fresh air. The winter sun was dull and silvery, the snow on the ground a layer of crunchy filth. When I saw somebody I knew I changed direction, convinced by the formlessness of my inner monologue that my linguistic incompetence had deepened. Just outside the gates, on Nassau Street, I stared into the window of a shop at a mannequin of a model undergraduate dressed in a toggled wool coat and a wool cap. The figure was holding an old edition of Fitzgerald's *This Side of Paradise*, which I understood—incorrectly, it turned out—to be a pure celebration of Princeton's goldenness. I wished I had money to buy the coat. It looked like a garment a boy could hide in, with a hood that would cast a shadow over his face and pockets in which to conceal his trembling hands.

Someone touched my right elbow: Adam. He spoke. I smiled. He spoke again, at length. I held the smile. His eyes narrowed with what I gathered to be concern. I rubbed my brow in some vague, all-purpose excuse, and before he could inquire further, I darted across the street and set a course toward the Princeton Theological Seminary, where I felt confident I'd be left alone. Wrong. While I was resting on a bench there, Professor R. appeared beside me. He gestured bizarrely with a bent thumb, scratching at the air.

He wanted something.

I figured it out when I saw his unlit cigarette.

He was the last person I wanted to see. A poet in the Creative Writing Department, Professor R. was my junior-paper adviser and my only real friend among the faculty. The purple dents beneath his eyes, his powerlessness over coffee and tobacco, and his kindly, doleful manner had persuaded me that I could trust him. It helped that he was in his early thirties and looked like a student, just a very tired one. We met periodically in his small office to review my progress on my paper about John

Berryman's *Dream Songs*, a harrowing cycle of poems about rage, but within a few minutes the topic usually shifted to something broader. These discussions allowed me to flourish arcane concepts picked up from my bull sessions with V., but if Professor R. ever caught on to the thinness of my borrowed ideas, he was careful not to show it. With him, I was the thinker I hoped to pass as, skeptical, ironic, and unconventional. We drank our coffee black with sugar and let the ashes from our waving cigarettes fall where they might, on the floor and on his desk.

There was a fair chance I loved the man.

I read his lips as he thanked me for a light. My "You're welcome," though scrambled to my own ears, didn't appear to alarm or disconcert him. His manner remained easy, casual. Judging by the shapes his mouth made and my memories of our last conference, I surmised that he was talking about Berryman; about his "melodic strategies," perhaps, or, it could have been, his "misanthropy." I devised a remark that allowed for most contingencies ("I'm still assessing that") and then, in response to the thoughtful-sounding statement which then came forth from him, I said, "My instinct is you're on the mark." Any further than this I couldn't go, though; my throat was swelling shut with panic. Worse, the faint creases between my teacher's eyebrows had darkened and turned severe, suggesting, perhaps, that I'd been sorely mistaken about the nature of his utterances. What if he'd been remarking on the weather?

I finessed an exit from the encounter, and over the next few days I taught myself how to disguise a fugue state while in public. The secret was to mirror others' expressions, not perfectly but approximately, scratching my forehead when they rubbed their chins or leaning back when they leaned to the side. Continuity was important, too. I had to maintain a flow of gestures that mimicked engagement, interest, and reflection, and I had to be sure not to freeze while choosing the next one. I learned that the more intently I seemed to listen, the less I would be expected to speak. Oddly, this caused people to open up to me. Friends who'd once seemed shy and awkward to me became loquacious and gregarious. It was as though by suppressing my own voice, I'd liberated theirs, and I saw in their faces a new affection for me. I noticed I was getting waves and winks from classmates who used to whisk past me with lowered heads.

I blamed my condition on exhaustion. One night I slept for twenty hours straight. When I finally got up, the floor felt like a waterbed; I had to brace myself against a chair. Then I heard vermin inside the walls. I knew that the noises came from warming water pipes, but I couldn't stop picturing whiskered rodents nibbling through the plaster into my room. Having slept through breakfast, lunch, and dinner, I made my way to a convenience store next to the train station at the edge of campus, but the profusion of snack foods on the shelves swamped my decision-making center. I returned empty-handed to my dorm.

My aphasia worsened by the day. Words were disappearing from my memory like defective bulbs in a strand of Christmas lights. The words didn't vanish in order of difficulty. One morning in the shower, swabbing my chest with a slick white lump of something, I lost track of "soap." At lunch at the Terrace Club "bread" and "vinegar" blinked out. But trickier words persisted. In a religion class one afternoon the professor wrote "telos" on the board. Easy. A synonym for "purpose." But what was the stick of plastic in my right hand? And what was the black stuff issuing from its tip?

For a few weeks I was still able to write, but it was a punishing, grim, self-conscious labor. I began most of my sentences with "the." Then I went looking for a noun. "The book" was often the result. Next, I seemed to remember, should come a verb. "Is" is a verb. It became my favorite verb. I liked it for its open-endedness—the way it allowed for a wide range of next moves. "The book is always . . ." "The book is thought to . . ." "The book is green and . . ." Impermissible. Yes, a book might be a certain color, but starting an essay with the fact wasn't what college was all about. What was it all about? It was about making statements that weren't obvious for people who made such statements professionally. "The book is a gestural construct possessed of telos."

There, I could rest. I'd done it. An hour's work.

As compensation for these agonies I allowed myself nights of immobility in the Terrace Club TV room. Other viewers came and went, squeezing in next to me on the crumbling sofa. They included a girl whose family had pioneered the African diamond-mining industry, lent their name to the nation of Rhodesia, and founded the Rhodes Scholarships. She seemed to like me, and I envisioned a marriage that would entitle me to a splendid estate. It wasn't a farfetched notion, either, for here she was, my princess, within arm's reach. And yet something kept me from pursuing her. It wasn't just my muteness. It was dread. Dread of exposure, of failure, and of collapse, but mostly dread of gaining what I sought (distinction, others' envy, the world itself) and discovering that it wasn't I who'd sought it.

My education was running in reverse as my mind shed its outermost layer of signs and symbols and shrank back to its dumb, preliterate core. I lay on my bed with a notebook at my side (in case my faculties suddenly returned) and tried to imagine a future for myself that wouldn't require verbal communication. Other than a job as a night watchman, I couldn't come up with anything. My dreams, when I finally managed to nod off, were full of sensory absurdities: handguns firing with cooing sounds, garden hoses spraying streams of sand. I woke after every one of them, woke fully, as though it were morning, time to wash and dress, and only by checking my watch (two thirty a.m.) did I manage to keep myself in bed. To fall back asleep, to relax, I had to smoke—a total of three or four cigarettes, most nights—and by sunrise my system was still so charged with nicotine that I had trouble handling a toothbrush. Soon streaks of blood appeared along my gum line, welling up into the cracks between my teeth and making me look like a wolf over a kill. I rinsed off the blood with Listerine, which stung, and then scourged my raw mucus membranes with yet more smoke, hungry for its noxious particles in a way that I no longer was for eggs and orange juice.

My breakdown climaxed with a strange prank that could have been taken straight from a bad novel about collegiate social Darwinism. I was watching TV in the Terrace Club library when in walked Leslie, a handsome blond campus prince—the descendant of a legendary industrialist—whom I knew to be one of the Joy Division's high chieftains but had never felt worthy of engaging in conversation.

"Walter, may I speak with you?" he said. I was astonished that he knew my name.

I followed him outside to his car, a new European sports coupe with leather seats, where he asked me to help him with a "trust experiment" related to one of his sociology classes. He couldn't describe the experiment, he said, because it might prejudice the results, and I didn't press him. I wanted him to like me. I wanted him to owe me, too, perhaps. Having someone like him in my debt, if only slightly, might come in handy someday, especially if I kept on deteriorating.

Leslie started the car as I buckled in next to him. His instructions were simple: don't speak and don't resist. Then he blindfolded me with a strip of fuzzy dark cloth. He turned on a Laurie Anderson tape full blast—a gale of futuristic electronica—and drove without stopping for what felt like an hour, ending up on a bumpy stretch of road that I took to be rural and remote. At some point my blindfold loosened and slipped down, and I resecured it without being asked. That's how trusting I wanted to appear.

The car stopped moving. The music ceased. Leslie got out, walked around to my side, opened the door, set his hands on my shoulders, and marched me forward across an expanse of spongy, uneven earth. He halted and commanded me to kneel, urging me down by pressing on my skull. I suspected by then that I'd been lured into a sadistic hazing ritual, but instead of lashing out or fleeing, I fantasized about the sort of club that I'd been deemed worthy of trying out for.

"Remove the blindfold," Leslie said.

When I raised my dazzled eyes, I saw, about fifty yards in front of me, surrounded by stately trees, an actual castle, with countless tall windows, pediments, and columns. In the center of its crescent driveway stood an enormous dry fountain of leaping cupids.

"My family's estate," said Leslie. "Behold, poor serf! Behold a power you will never know!"

With that he ran back to his car and drove away.

It took me three hours, walking and hitchhiking, to make it back to Princeton. The pills that I'd taken earlier with Adam turned the trip into an odyssey of spectral laughing faces in the sky and miasmic whirlpools underfoot. When I was finally safe inside my room, I asked myself why I'd been chosen for this elaborate torture session. I couldn't come up with a satisfying answer. Rumor had it that Leslie was gay, but he'd tried nothing physical with me. Maybe he'd planned to and chickened out. Or maybe, while I was wearing the blindfold and the music was roaring in the car, he'd unzipped his jeans and masturbated. There was also a chance he felt encroached upon. He considered himself a sort of Olympian overseer at the campus's hippest, most vicious student theater, and I'd been hanging out there fairly regularly, shooting the shit about plays I planned to write and my disagreements with Artaud, in the weeks before my cerebral crash. It hardly mattered, though. I burned with shame for bowing to his orders and blamed the pills, prescription opiates, for my craven passivity, though I knew that deep down the problem was ambition. The drugs I could cut down or give up, as I vowed to almost every weekend, but not the ambition. Not the itch, the push.

The next day, through Adam, I heard the story from Leslie's side. I learned that he'd been spreading lies. He'd said he'd seduced me in the woods. He said I'd been easy, agreeable, a pushover. This cruel tale incensed me. None of it was true. Neither, sadly, was it entirely false. I could dispute it on a literal level, but not on the allegorical, so I chose not to speak about it at all. This was wildly frustrating for me but not difficult, because by then I could barely speak my name. And now I didn't really want to.

# Fifteen

I CHOSE TO STAY IN PRINCETON FOR THE SUMMER RATHER
than go home and shock my family with my listlessness and dissipation. I rented a room with a cot at the Terrace Club and
took a job shelving books at Firestone Library. I also made a bargain with myself. If I couldn't rebuild my brain within three
months, I wouldn't register for my senior year. And if my state
worsened, I might kill myself. Should I decide that this was necessary, my model would be my favorite poet, John Berryman,
who'd spent time around Princeton in the fifties but ended up,
two decades later, in Minneapolis, teaching at the U of M,
where he leaped from a bridge into the Mississippi. According
to one account I'd heard, the river was covered with ice that
day, so he'd actually jumped onto it. Either way, he'd succeeded.
He met the silence.

Hoping to stave off this meeting, I bought a dictionary and
a thesaurus and instituted a daily regimen of linguistic calisthenics. My alarm clock woke me every morning at five, and for the
next three hours I'd lie in bed, with my reference books
propped open on my stomach, and repeat aloud, in alphabetical

order, every word on every single page, along with its defini-
tions and major synonyms. The ritual was humbling but sooth-
ing, and for the first time in my academic career I found myself
making measurable strides, however minuscule. "Militate."
"Militia." "Milk." I spent as much energy on the easy words as I
did on the hard ones—my way of showing contrition for squan-
dering my high-percentile promise. And in truth, they were all
hard words for me by then.

My job in the library basement helped advance this program of self-styled mental reconstruction. Working under a
young crew boss, Dan, who belonged to a self-improvement
cult masked as an end-hunger organization, I emptied one-
hundred-yard-long shelves of books, loaded them onto rolling
metal carts, and transferred them to new shelves, one floor
down, in perfect Dewey decimal order. When breaks were
called, I opened whichever volume I happened to be holding at
the moment and read until it was time to go to work again,
picking up reams of miscellaneous knowledge about such topics
as Zoroastrianism and the history of animal husbandry. And unlike the material from my classes and lectures, these fragments
stuck with me—maybe because I'd collected them for their own
sake, not as cards to be played at final-exam time and then forgotten when a new hand was dealt.

One day, during lunch, my boss sat down beside me while
I was reading up on Zarathustra, whom I'd known before then
only as a word in the title of a book by Nietzsche that I'd often
argued with V. about, despite never having gotten through the
preface.

"Personal self-betterment," said Dan. "That's man's purpose
on earth, you know."

I nodded.

"Do you understand the power of thought?"

"Not really."

"Thought is stupendous. Thought's a miracle. I'll give you an example. This really happened. There were some monkeys living on an island. They drank out of streams, with their faces in the water. Then one of them had a breakthrough, an idea. He dipped half a coconut shell into the stream and drank from it like a primitive cup. Pretty soon, all of the monkeys were doing it. The whole pack or gaggle or whatever."

"That's amazing," I said, not meaning it.

"No, it's not. The amazing part is this. There was another monkey island a hundred miles away across the ocean, and the minute the monkey on the first one learned to drink its water from the shell, the other monkey on the second island got it in his head to follow suit. The thought was transmitted through space, a kind of signal. We call that 'critical mass.'"

"Some scientist actually witnessed this?"

"You bet. Not that it was reported very widely."

"Why not? Because it wasn't true?" I couldn't help needling brainwashed Dan. I knew it wouldn't alter his beliefs, but now that I was struggling to think again, I couldn't let such nonsense pass.

"Can you come to a meeting of people who share your drive? It's absolutely free of charge," he said.

"I'm sorry. I have to do this thing alone."

"What thing?"

"Reconnecting certain wires."

Rebuffing Dan's invitation to join the cult harmed our re-lations. He hovered as I toiled, griping about my inefficient technique, and a couple of times he snatched my books away from me and showed me how I should carry and handle them so as to raise my rate of productivity. Whenever he caught me reading one of them, he reached out and slapped its cover shut, forcing me to conduct my hasty studies in unsupervised corners of the basement. Five minutes of peace was the most that I could hope for. But I adapted. The units were long enough. I stuffed my head with chunks of information that I knew I might never get to use—on medieval theology, general relativity, monastic architecture, Sir Walter Raleigh—and slowly displaced the vacuum in my skull.

A girl on the crew, a classmate, Kate, watched from afar as I toiled at my comeback. She was a Californian and a painter, an auxiliary member of the Joy Division who didn't entirely fit in because of her breezy, beachy temperament, which wasn't severe enough to impress the leadership. I liked her red hair. I liked its tumbling splendor. One night after work we went out for a beer.

"What's all the sneaking away about?" she asked me.

"I'm trying to pass a test."

"There aren't any tests. It's summer. It's a rest. You'll make yourself sick."

"I'm already pretty sick."

By fully confessing to my fatigue and speculating on its causes, I earned a few hours of messy groping that left me refreshed, if not proud of my performance. But Kate didn't seem to care about performance. Like me, she was hungry for company itself, for simple epidermal contact, as though her world, too, had dematerialized and needed replenishment by any means. We stuck close to each other in the library, exchanging glances that said merely "I'm here," and this elemental ex-change of presence placed a sort of floor under my sorrows. I wasn't sinking, for once. I wasn't slipping. Further support was provided by my readings. *Sons and Lovers* explores the Oedipus complex. Frank Lloyd Wright designed the Guggenheim. When Troilus died and left the earth after discovering Cressida's be-trayal, he floated up into the sky and gazed back down and laughed at the pitiful folly of human wishes. It was basic stuff, nothing arcane or glamorous, but it was substantial enough to set my feet on.

By August, I felt human again. The hollow sensation be-hind my forehead was replaced by a reassuring fullness. The tics and twitches subsided. My gums healed up. I realized that for several weeks I'd been conversing normally—with Kate, at least.

"How do I look?" I asked her. "Compared to then." She knew what I was referring to.

"You're thicker."

"Fatter?"

She shook her head. "Just thicker."

**A**nd then I wrote a three-act play—in verse. It took about two weeks, no more than that, and the process was more like flood control than ordinary composition. The lines surged out of me onto the page as though they'd been inside me all along, but the lexicon was new, I saw, drawn from my five-minute lessons in the library and blessedly free of theory terms. Where the play's subject came from I didn't know. The setting was a Manhattan artist's studio that resembled Andy Warhol's Factory, a messy crash pad for vagrant visionaries and a doomed teenage socialite named Dinah who, I suppose, was based on Edie Sedgwick, whose story I'd heard about from Adam. This crowd was alien to me, but no more so than the Joy Division. I called my main character "the Director." He didn't speak much, just lounged behind a movie camera, recording the love affairs, squabbles, and overdoses of his solipsistic groupies, who rarely acknowledged or even looked at him. I called the play *Soft White Kids in Leather*. No real reason. The title volunteered itself.

I sat at my desk in wonder the morning I finished, resting one hand atop the stacked white pages as though I were swearing on the Bible. I was afraid to reread the dialogue in case it made no sense. I took the manuscript downstairs to the dining room and waited for someone sane to come along who might be able to deem the thing intelligible, but when no one showed up, I took the play to work with me and showed it to Kate, who scanned a page or two and pronounced my creation "interesting," which was all the affirmation I needed. Suicide wouldn't be necessary, after all.

"**M**om?"

"Is everything okay?"

"I think so. I think it is. Is Dad there?"

"Fishing."

"Is Andy there?"

"Why? What's going on?"

"Say 'hi' to him."

"I don't like the sound of this call."

"Say 'hi' to everyone."

"You're all jazzed up. You're scaring me," she said.

"I'm rushing. I'm on a break. More books to shelve. Just wanted to phone and give everyone my love."

"Your 'love,' " my mother said suspiciously. It wasn't a word that we used much in our family. I must have stumbled across it in the library.

I treated myself to a pizza that night, a pie with everything on it except pineapple. I ate alone. Kate had gone back to California. Afterward, on Nassau Street, I returned to the storefront where I'd seen the toggle coat. The new display featured autumn back-to-school clothes. Corduroy pants. Shirts with alligator insignias. Belts of pebbly hide. I had the money to buy a couple of items, but I'd have to wait until the morning, and I knew that by then I'd lose my nerve. I'd saved myself, by all appearances, but suddenly a new concern arose. With graduation just a year away and no firm career plans or even career desires (my vague interests in drama and poetry didn't qualify), the only game I'd ever learned to play—scaling the American meritocratic mountain—was, I feared, about to end.

# Chapter Sixteen

MAKING MONEY DIDN'T INTEREST ME. WHILE MY CLASS-
mates signed up for on-campus "face-to-faces" with recruiters
from Wall Street brokerage firms (becoming an "arbitrageur"
was all the rage then, even among students who as juniors had
vowed to spend their lives dancing or composing), I scanned the
horizon for another test to take, another contest to compete in.
I hadn't learned any lessons from my breakdown. The curse had
me right back in its grip. Here I was, just this side of mental
paralysis, and again I was starving for medals, stars, acceptance
letters. To me, wealth and power were trivial by-products of
improving one's statistical scores in the great generational tournament of aptitude. The ranking itself was the essential prize.

I applied for two scholarships to Oxford, an institution I regarded much as I'd regarded Princeton once—as a sociocultural
VIP room that happened to hold classes in the back. The first
application was for the Rhodes, created to fashion leaders for a
future utopian global order dreamed of by the diamond-mining
magnate who'd passed down his genes to the girl in the TV
room whom I'd been too cowardly to court. Why I imagined

that I was "Rhodes material"—which at Princeton meant someone resembling Bill Bradley, our most widely known recipient of the honor—I had not a clue. The other kids I knew who had applied were conspicuous campus presences, top athletes and leaders of student government, whereas I was an addled loner in an old raincoat who'd burped out a blank-verse play on Andy Warhol that hadn't been staged yet and might never be, unless Adam dug up some funds for the production. I was also an unindicted vandal, a suspected offender against the Honor Code, a phony theory devotee, and a chain-smoking post-aphasic whose only bulwark against regression was a heavily underlined thesaurus.

Still, I felt I had an outside shot. I'd learned by then that the masters of advancement use a rough quota system in their work, reserving a certain number of wild-card slots for overreaching oddballs. I suspected that they only did this to keep more qualified candidates on their toes, but I also knew that an opening is an opening. Just get in the room, and then act like you belong there while cozying up to the folks who clearly do—this had always been my winning formula and I saw no good reason to abandon it.

To increase my chances of success, I made no contingency plans for failure. I threw myself on the mercy of the universe. V., who was seeking spots at various grad schools, cautioned me against overconfidence, but once I explained my superstitious reasoning—I wasn't showing confidence at all; I was soliciting an act of grace—he backed me up by citing Kierkegaard, a Danish philosopher of the nineteenth century who'd argued that faith in the divine makes sense only because it makes no sense whatsoever. Hearing my position thus affirmed should have heartened me, but it made me antsy. Philosophers weren't reliable authorities on how to operate in the real world. Indeed, if you found yourself acting in accordance with one of their mad principles, it was probably wisest to change course.

When a letter arrived to tell me I'd been chosen as one of about a dozen state finalists, I prayerfully thanked the god of desperadoes, bought a blue suit at the store on Nassau Street, and flew back to Minnesota for my interview. I told a flight attendant on the plane that I'd already secured the prize—this to preview the awe I might expect if I ever really did. The woman poured me a Pepsi and moved along.

An hour after I landed, a doorman at the Minneapolis Club showed me upstairs to a gloomy paneled lounge where my name-tagged fellow aspirants were enjoying a get-acquainted party with the distinguished members of the committee that would formally screen us the next morning. I armed myself with a cheese cube on a napkin and a glass of red wine and strode into the fray, looking for someone important to impress, but my rivals had gotten the jump on me and wouldn't loosen the tight perimeters around the professors and businesspeople tasked with assessing our leadership potential. To my mind, the vaunted mission of the Rhodes smacked of a sort of science-fiction Nazism, but perhaps because it hadn't yet borne fruit in the form of a smarty-pants universal directorate (and because it paid for swank gatherings such as this one), no one had seen fit to put a stop to it.

I poured myself a second glass of wine and went on circling the inner circle. Seeing my rivals up close unsettled me. Back when I took the SATs, the contest had been abstract, statistical, waged against an anonymous national peer group that was no more real to me than the tens of thousands of other nine-year-olds vying for the presidential fitness prize. But this time the competition was all too personal. One short-haired young woman in a pressed dark suit was holding forth on national health-care policy to a man who kept peeking past her at a prettier girl whose panty lines were vivid through her dress. A crew-cutted young roughneck whose tag identified him as a West Point cadet was describing his diet and fitness regimen to a lady who seemed to be sleeping standing up. Every few minutes everyone changed partners, like dancers in a Jane Austen ballroom scene. What expert mixers they were! I hated them.

Then I noticed something more disturbing: the other contestants weren't drinking their wine. They were using their glasses as props, as things to gesture with.

I looked down at my empty goblet. Caught out again.

By the time I succeeded in cornering a committee member, I was feeling squirrelly and light-headed. To give the irresistible impression of humble origins transcended, I affected a lazy backwoods drawl and combined it with a Sunday-best vocabulary garnered from my brain-restoring drills. I even got off the word "heuristic" once, an elegant bit of scholastic legerdemain, but I pronounced it in the manner of Johnny Cash. I knew I sounded demented, but by then I'd committed to the performance and feared that shifting to another register would only compound the impression of schizophrenia. The best I could do was gradually fall silent and pretend to be an avid listener. That, and refrain from lighting another cigarette. Besides being the party's only young drinker, I was its only smoker, it turned out, aside from a bearded old fellow with a pipe whose name tag marked him as an English professor at a local college,

Carleton. I approached him, seeking cover for my vice, and babbled away about my love of Whitman, a name I'd plucked out of the air. He seemed to sense this.

"What about Whitman do you admire?" he asked me.

"Well, his first name for one thing."

"Why?"

"I'm kidding. Because it's my name. Walt." I tapped my name tag for proof. The old man squinted. I wondered what qualified him as a Rhodes judge. Not his powers of observation, surely. Some feeling that only an engineered elite could rescue humanity from doom?

"Actually, I admire his populist empathy. Dockworkers, farmers, soldiers—he loved them all."

"But did he just love them as aspects of Walt Whitman? He called the poem 'Song of Myself,' remember."

"Right."

"And you wrote a poem once, at Macalester College, for which you won a prize, and which we've read, because you submitted it in your application, called 'From an Uncolored Room.'"

I confessed the truth of this.

"Enlightening chat. Quite helpful. Good luck, young man."

At the end of the cocktail party we drew times for our morning interviews. I drew the very first slot: seven sharp. I showed up white and trembling and dehydrated, speckled with crumbs from a cherry Danish I'd wolfed. My rivals were already seated in the waiting room, some of them paging through *The New York Times*, one of them filling out the last few squares of its famously challenging crossword puzzle, which he must have begun long before he reached the club. This was a stroke I wished I'd thought of, though I would have handled it slightly differently. I would have put random letters in the squares, since who was going to check?

My name was called and I sat down in a conference room at a long table of grim interrogators equipped with pencils, clipboards, and questionnaires. "What, in your opinion," one woman asked me, not even giving me time to sip my coffee, "is the primary problem facing our world today?"

The moisture returned to my mouth, but it was sour, as though mucus membranes can perspire, too. I'd expected a little small talk first. I knew in my gut that to answer the question creatively would be a mistake; these were sober, high-minded people who'd woken up early to serve the citizenry by preselecting future American presidents and United Nations ambassadors. The only issues worthy of their seriousness, I strongly suspected, were the obvious two: poverty and war. My chance to show originality would come with the inevitable follow-up: "And how would you deal with this problem?" That's where the challenge lay. I wanted to bring in poetry—but how? By calling for a new, transformative literature pledged to the empowerment of the voiceless through a concern with the universal values of justice and mutual respect?

That might be a winner, if I could just remember it.

But I couldn't remember anything. All I could think about were the other applicants pretending to read their papers in the lounge while secretly wishing an epileptic fit on me. I could feel their ill will oozing in under the door. I could feel the high-pressure cell of their massed ambition pressing against the hinges of the door.

"Miscommunication would be my answer."

Horrible. But my ad-lib would have to stand.

"Expand on that, please," said a quiet female voice as pens began scratching across important papers. "Miscommunication among whom?"

I offered a roster of miscommunicators that included governments and their subjects, men and women, adults and children, and even—absurdly—human beings and animals. Halfway through my speech I knew I'd lost. Aside from the presidential rope climb, I'd never lost at anything before except for a spelling bee in Phoenix, and the feeling was like waking on the moon after having gone to bed on earth. I left my body. Or maybe my body left me. They zoomed away in opposite directions, with only an echoing "human beings and animals" indicating the spot which they'd once shared.

I returned to the waiting room ten minutes later, after a ceremonial round of questions about my beliefs as a "young artist." My rivals scanned my face for clues: How had my interview changed the odds for them? I gave them more information than they deserved, hoping to win their favor for the future. Someday one of them might rule all earth, and I wanted to be remembered as a good sport.

"You're safe," I announced to all of them. "I blew it."

"How?" said someone, eager for a tip.

"Don't worry. It's only going to happen once today."

My competitors couldn't help grinning. Then one girl hugged me—the health-care expert, whom I realized I'd known at Macalester, back when. "You really shouldn't consider it a loss," she said. "You should feel honored that you reached this level."

I returned the hug against my will, my desire for pity prevailing over my dignity. Then I turned away and left the building, unwilling to wait for the winners to be named. Later I learned that the health-care girl was one of them—one of only two Rhodes from our home region—which made her gesture seem false in retrospect. She knew she was bound for the sharp end of the pyramid, and was merely rehearsing her royal manners.

"Is this Walter Kirn?" asked the phantom of Nassau Hall.

"It is," I said. "It's him." Anxiety over poor grammar ensures poor grammar.

"The provost would like to meet with you next week about a confidential matter. Would Wednesday at noon work?"

"Any time would work. May I ask you a question?"

"Please," the ghost said.

"How bad is it?"

"It's good."

The meeting spot was a modest diner across the street from Princeton's grand front gate. A letter I'd received the day before explained why I'd been summoned: to talk about another overseas scholarship, less coveted than the Rhodes but more exclusive (only a handful were awarded each year) sponsored by the Keasbey Foundation, an organization based in Philadelphia. I'd applied for the Keasbey at the urging of a junior English professor, the cheerful medievalist whom I was fond of because he paused between his sentences and went light on theory. He'd won the Keasbey himself a few years back and thought it the finest scholarship on offer because it gave winners a choice of universities—not just Oxford, but also Cambridge, Edinburgh, and even Aberystwyth, in Wales—as well as supplying a generous "wine allowance" of a few hundred dollars per year. I asked why this was. "It's in the will," he said. I asked him whose will. "Marguerite Keasbey's."

I ordered a BLT and perched on a stool in the window of the diner, wondering how I'd recognize a being whose title had always been a cipher to me. It was easy, though. Provosts behave exactly like provosts. They shake your hand a moment before you're ready, they lay a heartening arm across your shoulder that drops away the instant you feel heartened, they lightly scold you for using your own money to buy your BLT, and they don't touch their coffee after the first sip because they're granting you their full attention, which they somehow convince you that you deserve.

"The first round of judging for the Keasbey is done by the university itself. That process has been concluded. Concluded in your favor, I'm pleased to say." He brought out a sheaf of neatly folded documents and slid it across the Formica toward my plate, a gesture familiar from movies about espionage. I followed what I gathered to be the script and immediately tucked the papers out of sight, in a pocket of my jeans.

"Don't lose those. Make sure to read them," the provost said. "They contain details on next week's interview."

"I'm grateful. Thank you, sir. Sincerely. Wow."

"You don't want to read them now and ask some questions?"

"Is that what you want?"

"It's whatever you want."

"Really?"

The provost accompanied me back to campus, a ghostly red carpet unfurling before him that I was allowed to set my feet on, too. People waved at him, people I'd never seen before. I imagined that they were deans, administrators, and I wondered through what quirk of quantum physics they'd suddenly managed to gain materiality. At the foot of the staircase to Nassau Hall's front doors, watched by the twin bronze tigers, who were purring now, I received a second provostian handshake, a second fleeting shoulder clasp, and then he was gone, in a twinkling, my own Saint Nicholas, traveling undercover in a brown suit. I touched the papers in my back pocket. Real.

The euphoria only lasted a few minutes. In my dorm room, I sat down on my bed next to the leafless potted plant in which I sometimes urinated when the hike to the men's room felt too long, and handicapped my chances in the last round. The Rhodes debacle had broken my confidence, but rather than learning from it the obvious lesson—that I should prepare for auditions before the wise ones—I doubled up on my old strategy of conjuring mercy through helplessness and squeezing inspiration from despair. I drifted through my classes the next day, and every day for the next week, astonished anew by how little four years of college had affected me. The great poems and novels mystified me still, particularly the ones I'd written papers on, and my math skills, once adequate for the SATs, had atrophied to nothing. The science classes I'd been required to take, on geology and psychology, had been graded pass-fail, and though I'd passed them, barely, I'd already forgotten what "igneous" meant and where in the brain short-term memories were stored.

Worse, I had no prospects. All around me friends were taking positions with worldwide corporations and securing places in lofty grad schools, but I had nothing but three sheets of paper, one of them mapping the quickest route from Princeton to downtown Philadelphia, the site of my upcoming ultimate rebuff. I'd never bothered to contemplate the moment when the quest for trophies would end, as would the game of trading on previous trophies. Once I had nowhere to go but up. Now I had nowhere to go at all, it seemed. The only suspense was what shape defeat would take. There he goes, the Ivy League grocery bagger. There he lies, the hobo with the diploma.

"Stop it," said V. during one of my moping orgies. My interview was just two days away. "This is unwarranted. And it's beneath you."

"It isn't Kierkegaardian? No, you're right. It's Schopenhauerian."

"The fact that you can even make such jokes means that you've come further than you know."

"But you're the only person I can make them to. They're good for another few months, until we leave here, and then I'll be all alone with them," I said.

"You don't know what 'all alone' means, obviously."

"What? It means something different in Pakistan?"

V. nodded. Not immediately, reluctantly. Then he folded his hands and stared down into his lap. He seemed disappointed in me, or in our friendship. I began to understand. His time here was precious, he'd stolen it from his government, and he'd paid for it with a separation. The fact that he'd spent so much of it with me—who not only didn't appreciate the privilege but didn't appreciate anything, apparently, beginning with himself—must have struck him as a ghastly waste.

# Seventeen

I RODE DOWN TO PHILADELPHIA WITH PRINCETON'S OTHER Keasbey nominee, the starting quarterback of the varsity football team. I'd never expected to meet him in this life. He was smaller than I thought he'd be and a sharper, more impressive talker. Under his short haircut he seemed sad, though, as if he, too, were confronting the possibility that his young life had climaxed in some way. His car was old, with poor radio reception, not a quarterback's car at all, and I realized that he wasn't one anymore, except in memory. The season had ended several weeks ago, and Ivy League football players seldom ever went pro. As my father had, they played for parchment, for degrees they might not have been eligible for otherwise. Then they tucked them under their arms and ran.

"Thanks for the lift," I kept saying as we drove on. I meant it, too. I liked the guy. He had the reflexive politeness of college athletes who are obliged to kiss up to rich alumni, but his willingness to do a rival a service—on the morning of a game day, no less—was evidence of something beyond good sportsmanship. It spoke of serenity, a mellow fatalism. Fortune was going to speak in a few hours, but until then he planned to leave things to themselves, which isn't how quarterbacks are meant to think.

We parked downtown and followed the provost's map to a stony office building, past whose revolving door and up whose elevators was the main office of the law firm which administered the Keasbey Trust. In the stodgy reception room we met our adversaries—five or six students from the other top colleges that the fellowship's snobby benefactress had deemed worthy of sharing in her legacy. The tension I'd felt at the Rhodes assembly was absent, perhaps because there was less prestige at stake. The world didn't know that we were there, and the newspapers wouldn't publish the results.

A secretary led us to a larger room, where the trustees were sitting at a table that had been waxed and buffed and waxed again, for decades and perhaps for centuries, until the shine was thicker than the wood. Most of the trustees were older men, their faces soft with patience and good humor. I felt instantly comfortable with them, convinced that, unlike the tribunes of the Rhodes, they'd long ago abandoned any notion that society could be perfected or that the world had any single great problem—let alone one that a squad of model citizens could sally forth and solve. Indeed, the professor I knew who'd held the fellowship had told me that it wasn't for eager beavers, whiz kids, or perfectionists, but "interesting individuals." I asked him to be more specific, but he demurred. He said only, "They'll tell you when you get there. You have a treat in store."

The proceedings began with a lengthy presentation by the water-sipping head trustee, who spoke in the fashion of a medieval sheriff reading out tax rolls in a public square. His dry style didn't suit the narrative—the astonishing life and most peculiar last wishes of Miss Marguerite Keasbey, the spinster heiress to a vast asbestos fortune—but it did render certain details a bit more credible and help to satisfy us, his dumbstruck audience, that we still resided in present-day America and hadn't passed through a portal to Dickens's England.

The saga wasn't structured as a saga but it quickly became one in the mind, after the footnotes, digressions, summaries, and boilerplate legalisms were thrown away. It opened at a spring formal held in the gardens of an Oxford college. The blushing Miss Keasbey was new to such occasions, but not so new to them, one gathered, was the gallant British undergraduate who strode with her arm in arm onto the dance floor and showed her the time of her life, quite literally, because she not only remembered the dashing bachelor throughout her sojourn on this earth, she gave instructions when she left this earth on how to continually resurrect him. This would be done by funding a fellowship, complete with ample wine allowance, for the education of young Americans who, with the proper training, Miss Keasbey hoped, might someday wear her escort's cummerbund.

End of Part One. We were asked if we had questions. We certainly did, as the trustee surely knew, but perhaps too many to ask. If I could have asked only two, they would have been: "Is that really Philadelphia out the window?" and "Why do people bother to write novels?"

Part Two of the presentation was not as colorful, but it was just as melancholy, for it spoke of the age-old losing battle that romance wages against reason. Miss Keasbey had plainly stated in her will that her largesse was to go to males exclusively, but a court challenge waged in the name of civil rights had made young women eligible, too. The trustee didn't mask his displeasure with this travesty, this trespass against exquisite private fantasy by thuggish public interest, but there it was, and there it would remain. The old man grimaced and fell silent. He seemed to be reproaching us, and the girls among us most of all. Ours was a low and literal generation. In the name of equality we'd murdered fantasy. In our rush for a place in the sun, we'd stamped out the moonlight.

He seemed to be offering us a chance to leave, to confess our unworthiness and go—everyone but the prince who knew he was a prince, everyone but the disguised young Lancelot who'd traveled here not to win advancement in the sorry modern quest for status that had replaced the chivalric jousts of Camelot but because he'd been beckoned in a vision by a pale maiden clad in finest asbestos.

That's when I started to pity the other applicants. That's when I recognized them as impostors. They didn't belong here, and soon they'd be cast out, leaving behind them nothing but glasses of ice water. Because despite what the trustee went on to tell us about the supposed fairness of the judging ("Miss Keasbey's original wishes notwithstanding, you'll all be given the same consideration"), I knew that there would be no judging, really.

There would be a homecoming. A welcoming.

Because the true mad knight could only be me.

The trustees interviewed the ex-quarterback first, which gave me time to work on my persona as a ramshackle budding ladies' man whose intelligence was instinctive rather than practiced and whose sense of adventure had sometimes harmed him but not enough to cause him deep regrets. If my schooling had taught me anything, it was how to mold myself—my words, my range of allusions, my body language—into whatever shape the day required, but now, I sensed, I faced a different challenge: to put forth an ideal version of my real nature.

It worked. I could do no wrong that afternoon. I was in a state of grace. When one of the trustees brought up my D in Spanish—that glaring stain on my academic record, which the Rhodes committee had also noted, provoking in me much defensive stuttering—I confessed that I'd stayed up late drinking before the final and let it go at that. This elicited grins and merry twinkles. When they asked me about my athletic interests—or, rather, my apparent lack thereof—I replied that I like to exert myself in solitude, by taking long, meditative evening walks. "Very British," said one trustee. When they asked me who my favorite author was, I replied without hesitation: Lord Byron, as much for the life he'd led as for his writing. And when, toward the end, they asked me, hypothetically, how I would occupy myself abroad during the breaks between academic terms, I said, "I don't believe in planning vacations. I believe in taking them."

"What a pleasure. We thank you," the head trustee said. "I'm sure there's much more we could chatter on about, but I'm afraid others are patiently waiting their turns and we've run over time. By quite a bit."

I rose and moved down the table, shaking hands, and all of the handshakes felt like secret handshakes, as though we were exchanging palmed golden tokens. It appeared I'd come through, and by doing what I did best: treating the room as a text and reading it, first to myself and then aloud, to everyone. But this time I'd done it openly, not furtively. Because this time—a time that I thought would never come—it wasn't mastery they wanted but a certain vain and errant daring.

They wanted a hustler. They wanted an impressionist. They wanted someone to play a man of mystery who'd caught the fancy of a fool. And soon I'd be off to Oxford as a result. "Result" was not exactly the right word, though, because it suggested that logic governs destiny. But now I knew otherwise. Imagination does. And though part of me had always suspected as much and certain teachers had coached me in the notion ("Imagine that you can be anything you want"), what I hadn't understood at all was that our imaginations don't act alone. One's own imagination is powerless until it starts dancing with another's.

Imagine having been imagined. Imagine.

I couldn't. I hadn't. Perhaps because none of my teachers since Uncle Admiral—in whose imagination I'd been born, but whom I hadn't thought about for years; too busy—had told me that such duets were even possible. No wonder I'd grown so self-pitying and isolated. And no wonder I'd hated Princeton, that dreamland that seemed to dream only about itself (and asked that the world and its students do the same). But then, in Philadelphia, at what seemed to me like the last minute and in the most outlandish fashion, I discovered the truth—if words like "truth" mean anything. And even if they don't, perhaps.

Pause in your knowing to be known. Quit pushing—let yourself be pulled. Stop searching, frantic child, and be found.

Some call this Grace.

I called it Marguerite.

It came for me when I was alone and had no plans, asking for nothing but my company, and in return it offered to cover my studies, fill my wineglass, and teach me how to dance.

# Eighteen

A COUPLE OF WEEKS BEFORE I GRADUATED AND ONLY THREE months before I left for Oxford, my mother called to let me know that Uncle Admiral was ailing and that it might buoy him to see me and hear my thrilling news. I knew she'd always sent him Christmas cards and that he occasionally returned the favor by putting in the mail some trinket he'd made by hand. I'd seen a few of them. A Chinese ideogram for luck or happiness soldered together from scraps of silver. An Eisenhower dollar which had been cut away around Ike's profile and fitted with an eyelet so it could be worn as a medallion. Both pieces were chunky, odd, not terribly fetching, and wound up buried in a drawer.

"Spend a day with him. Tell him what you're up to. You know how he felt about London," my mother said.

"I was four. I don't remember now."

" 'If you're tired of London, you're tired of life.' "

"He got that from Dr. Johnson. Samuel Johnson. Eighteenth-century essayist and wit."

"I don't care where he got it. Get on a train."

He picked me up at the station in D.C. in his most recent Mercedes diesel. Back when, he'd bought a new one every few years, but this one had deeply seamed and wrinkled seats, some of them repaired with tape. But there was a compass on the dash, as usual, mounted up high and polished with Windex, and the floor mats had been vacuumed spotless. He looked old, but no older than before, when he'd already struck me as ancient, even immortal.

"We'll drink some Chock Full o'Nuts with cake," he said.

Until we reached his apartment, that was all he said. I sensed I was still a little boy to him and that he could only picture doing now exactly what we'd done back then. I guessed right. We sat in his kitchen at a small old table that had to be the same one, because why buy a second small old table. He sliced the pound cake with a butter knife and served me the slice I'd remembered: thick enough, but no more than enough. The chicory coffee in my mug stirred memories: of drinking chicory coffee. I looked around for other links to memory but the place, as before, was sparsely decorated—to the point of bleakness, I now felt. But maybe the feeling was unfounded. I'd been living in awfully grand surroundings lately.

"I won a nice fellowship, Uncle Admiral. To Oxford. I know how you always loved London."

"I did," he said. He turned his fork on its side above his plate and cut off a square from a corner of his cake. A perfect square, of one square inch. His mood was flat and hard to gauge. It had probably been that way when I was small, but when I was small I'd had no cause to gauge it. I was his pupil, he loved me, he loved the world, and he loved "mankind," his name for the great community of dreamers whose dreams, with his own, had sent him out to sea, to map the boundaries of the dreams. What did his mood matter in all of this?

"I like to dunk my pound cake in my coffee now." This was new. He showed me how he did it. I smiled and did it the same way. We weren't going to talk much, it was growing clear. But we'd done all our talking, so it was fine with me. I hadn't come here to talk. Or even to listen. I'd come here just to be here.

And then, at sixteen hundred hours—to give himself time to mix his daily cocktail and sit on the lawn chair in the yard from which he could see across the river to the white tip of his favorite obelisk—he drove me back to the station and said, "Safe trip."

As I rode home on the train, I read a copy of the letter Uncle Admiral had sent for me to the Rhodes Committee and gave to me as I left his apartment.

I am pleased to support the application of Walter N. Kirn III for a Rhodes Scholarship.

I have known the applicant since he was a babe in arms and during the first four or so years of his life was his surrogate father. From the time Walter could talk it was evident to me that he was a child of great potential and with a span of attention of great length. Many examples of precocity could be cited, perhaps one will suffice: when Walter was about five years old, I gave him a slide rule and in one lesson of an hour or less taught him to use it in multiplication and division.

Walter is personable in appearance, enjoys excellent health, and is modest about his scholastic accomplishments. If accepted in the Rhodes program I am certain that he will be a great credit to Princeton University and the United States.

Very truly yours,
Robert W. Knox
RADM USC&GS (Ret.)


That summer I found myself back home, drinking beer with an old high-school friend in a pickup truck parked next to the river. His name was Karl, and he'd stuck around the area to lend a hand on his family's dairy farm. Most everyone else from our crowd had moved away, part of the ongoing small-town diaspora that may someday depopulate much of rural America and in some districts already has. Our old buddies had mostly gone down to the Twin Cities, but some had gone farther. They did different things. They dealt cards in Las Vegas. They sold Toyotas in Denver. Some, having grown up with low-wage shift work, were studying computer programming or starting small businesses with borrowed money. I had a hard time envisioning their lives, especially if they'd married and had kids, but I didn't have to: they were gone. I'd gone away, too, up a ladder into the clouds. Up a ladder made of clouds. And thanks to the miracle of Miss Keasbey's will, a cloud had appeared that I might be able to stand on.

"So what are your views on Emerson?" Karl asked me.

We'd been discussing books, at his request. He'd looked me up that night for this very purpose. While I'd been off at Princeton, so busily polishing my act that I wore right through it and it cracked, he'd become a tireless reader as well as a devoted Buddhist. He said he had no one to talk to now, no one who shared his interest in art and literature and the "way of non-attachment," so when he'd heard I'd be home for a few months before moving to England, he'd driven right over. We had a great deal in common, Karl said.

But we didn't, in fact, or much less than he assumed, and I didn't know how to tell him this. To begin with, I couldn't quote the transcendentalists as accurately and effortlessly as he could. I couldn't quote anyone, reliably. I'd honed other skills: for flattering those in power without appearing to, for rating artistic reputations according to academic fashions, for matching my intonations and vocabulary to the backgrounds of my listeners, for placing certain words in smirking quotation marks and rolling my eyes when someone spoke too earnestly about some "classic" or "master-piece," for veering left when the conventional wisdom went right and then doubling back if it looked like it was changing.

Flexibility, irony, self-consciousness, contrarianism. They'd gotten me through Princeton, they hadn't quite kept me out of Oxford, and these, I was about to tell my friend, were the ways to get ahead now—not by memorizing old Ralph Waldo. I'd found out a lot since I'd aced the SATs, about the system, about myself, and about the new class that the system had created, which I was now part of, for better or for worse. The class that runs things.

But I kept all this to myself; I didn't tell Karl. He was a reader, a Buddhist, and an old pal, and there were some things he might not want to know. I wasn't so sure I wanted to know them either.


**M**y cynicism was creeping back, but later that summer something happened that changed me—not instantly but decisively. A few weeks before I was scheduled to fly to Scotland to spend a few days before I started at Oxford (Adam was staging *Soft White Kids in Leather* in a secondary venue at the Edinburgh Festival), I came down with a drippy summer cold that lingered, festered, and turned into pneumonia, forcing me to spend ten days in bed inside a fog bank of mentholated steam. One feverish night I found myself in the living room standing before the bookcase containing my mother's classics for the masses. I'd passed right by them a thousand times, scanned their titles no more than once a year, skimmed a couple of them, finished just one (and hilariously misread it—*The Great Gatsby*), but that night, bored and sick, I took one down and held it tight: *The Adventures of Huckleberry Finn*. Then I did something unprecedented for me: I carried it to my steamy bedroom and actually let it absorb me, page by page, chapter by chapter, straight on to the end. A few days later I repeated the feat with *Great Expectations*, another canonical stalwart that I'd somehow gotten through Princeton without opening. Shockingly, I already knew the story: Miss Havisham, a lunatic old woman, is thought to be the secret patron of Pip, the waifish boy who becomes a London gentleman.

And so, belatedly, haltingly, accidentally, and quite implausibly and incredibly, it began at last: my education. I wasn't sure what it would get me, whose approval it might win, or how long it might take to complete (forever, I had an inkling), but for once those weren't my first concerns. Alone in my room, congested and exhausted, I forgot my obsession with self-advancement. I wanted to lose myself. I wanted to read. Instead of filling in the blanks, I wanted to be a blank and be filled in.

I wanted to find out what others thought.